# A MARINE'S LETTERS:
# WORLD WAR II AND
# THE
# KOREAN WAR

## By
## Sgt. Fred T. Klemm, USMCR

Notes and bibliography
by
Florence F. Klemm

Colohi Productions
P.O. Box 8222
Colorado Springs, CO
80933-8222

Photo on p. 103 from <u>Leatherneck</u> magazine, July 1951. Reprinted with permission.

Klemm, Fred T., 1916-
    A Marine's letters:  World War II and the Korean War/by Sgt. Fred T. Klemm, USMCR.  187 p. 21.5 cm. illus., bibliog., index. Notes and bibliography by Florence F. Klemm.  Colorado Springs, CO: Colohi Productions, 1993.
1.      World War, 1939-1945-Pacific Ocean.
2.      World War, 1939-1945-Personal narratives, American.
3.      Korean War, 1950-1953-Personal narratives, American.
4.      United States.  Marine Corps-History-World War, 1939-1945.
5.      United States.  Marine Corps-History -  Korean War- 1950-1953.
VE 25 .K63
Cataloging supplied by the publisher.
ISBN 0-9635729-1-1

Cover photo:  three Presidential Unit Citations; two Navy unit citations; Asiatic Pacific Campaign ribbon with one engagement star; WWII Victory ribbon; China Service ribbon; Korea service ribbon with three engagement stars; Asiatic Pacific Campaign medal; WWII Victory medal; China Service medal.

Printed by Walsworth Publishing Co.

Price:  $15 plus $2 postage.
                Colohi Productions
                P.O. Box 8222
                Colorado Springs, CO
                80933-8222

## CONTENTS

Pfc. Fred T. Klemm, 1944

## Introduction

Fred T. Klemm was born in 1916 on his grandparents' homestead in Arkansas. He was the oldest of nine children, and when he was a young boy, the family moved to Texas where his father was a tenant farmer. Fred often worked to help support the family. They moved to Denver, Colorado in 1931. His parents were strict and fundamentalist Christians. It was at a church service that he met his future wife, Louella Mae Jones of Kansas. When they married in 1938, Fred was employed as a bus driver and custodian for the Denver Public Schools. Their daughter, Ethel, was born in 1939, and Florence was born in 1942.

Fred received his draft notice in 1943 and joined the Marines. Several years after the war, he composed this journal from the letters he had sent to his wife. In it he describes a different world, one which he hadn't expected. This was before the movies portrayed anything close to reality when it came to military life, a time when radio programs and movies were censored for language and content.

Fred's family: Ethel, Louella Mae, Florence, 1944

Theatre at San Diego MCB, with camouflage paint

Boot Camp platoon

# Chapter 1:  Boot Camp

Dec. 28, 1943.  Los Angeles, California, train 19.  Doing OK.  Lots of snow.  Trains not so bad.  I thought I would be able to string off quite a yarn, but can't think of anything at present.

Dec. 30, 1943.  Platoon 1204 San Diego Marine Corps Base, San Diego, 41, California. Private Fred T. Klemm.  Don't have much time.  Things are happening too fast.  It's a great life if you can take it; I'm not sure I can. I'm going to give it a good try.  The guy that said San Diego is warm is nuts.  I saw my first blimp the other day; saw the ocean from the train.  Don't know how often I can write you but don't worry--I'll be all right.  They're tough but they take good care of us.

 Tell my little girls I miss them.

Dec. 31, 1943.  I seem to be getting along pretty well.  At least I haven't been put on bread and water yet.  Got my hair cut today, and got a lot of other stuff including my rifle and bayonet.  I live in a hut, sleep in a sack, the toilet is the head. Walls are bulkheads, floor or ground is the deck.

 So much is happening to me, I can't begin to tell you everything.  You should get the allotment by the 15th of Jan.  You will get paid for December the same as me.  This platoon I'm in is made up mostly of Texans.  We were issued fur-lined vests because we couldn't stand the colder weather, ha, ha.  It felt good just the same.  This platoon will be broken up in seven weeks from January 1st. Looks like I'll land in the engineers.

Jan. 2, 1944.  It seems as how we are supposed to get a little time off today.  I thought we were going to get to go to church today, but the time came right at chow time.  For the Protestants, that is.  The Catholics went later.  Oh, well, I never was much for going to church anyway.  But for some reason or other you think different of it here.  The Marines are OK.  I just hope I can make it.  It is so different from anything I have ever heard of before.

 These Texans are nuts.  If you think I can tell some tall ones, you should hear some of the tales they tell, in what time we do have.

 I still have a lot to do even though it is Sunday.  Two pairs of shoes to shine, and I also have to cut off my dress pants one-half inch.  I have to memorize the General Orders and Position of Attention.  Must have recited them to the Drill Instructor by Wednesday. Hope I make it.

There are 61 men in this platoon.  Two or three can't read or write.  But they don't hold it against them; they just send them to school and teach them how.

There's so much to tell and I can't tell it all.  They have kept us so busy I didn't miss my family until last night.  Then it hurt.

Had police duty yesterday.  (Cleaning the head and picking up trash in the yard.)  Smoked my last cigarette last Wednesday. Couldn't get any more so I quit.  Don't send me any; I can't take care of them.  My sea bag is full now.


Jan. 4, 1944.  They're really putting us through the grind.  Got a few minutes off tonight.  I broke down Monday morning, mentally I mean.  The doctors called it mental hysteria.  I sat in the doctors' office and cried like a baby for over two hours.  But don't worry--it's all right now.  I've got to make good even if it is tough.

Don't have time to write to everyone I'd like to.  I signed the insurance papers.  In case of my death you will receive $10,000.

There are ten of us who can't swim 50 yards, so they start teaching us how to swim tomorrow.  We eat good here but have to do it pretty fast.  There's never enough time.  I'm having a hard time getting into the manual of arms.  We went over the obstacle course yesterday.  I made it--but--I was tired.

They don't ask us if we want to do anything; they just start the platoon marching and when we get there, we find out what we are going to do.  None of us can do anything without permission and then we all do it as a platoon.

When they show news reels here, they don't cut anything out.  I thought I'd throw up all over the place.

These Texans and that one from Montana are crazy.


Jan. 5, 1944.  Well, what do you know?  We get about four hours to ourselves.  But we have a lot of personal things to take care of during that time:  cleaning our rifles, polishing our shoes, washing, ironing, etc.  We get our first inspection Friday.  They began to teach us how to swim today.  We'll either learn how or die trying. I need some razor blades; I can't get them here.  I need a small pocket knife.  I had to send the one I have home because the blade was more than two inches long.  I can't use chewing gum or chewing tobacco or snuff.  I can have candy only if I receive enough for 60 men, the number in my platoon.

I'm beginning to get a kick out of this now.  It looks like I'm going to make it after all.  I just couldn't get into the swing of things at first.  I've been taking it too easy too long, I guess.

These Marines are plenty tough.  They wouldn't talk to a dog the way they talk to us--they'd just shoot it.

We've been hearing guns going off every now and then.  Since we couldn't see them, we wondered what they were.  We got up some nerve and asked the D.I.  He says they are A.A. (anti-aircraft) guns and they weren't being fired just to let us know what they sounded like.  Before the dim-out was lifted on the coast, they had smudge pots all over the place and kept smoke all over the base at all times.  You should see how they have everything hidden and painted.  This is a grim war in this part of the country.

Everything here has to be done on the double-time.  They want us to get used to quick movement in case a Jap should get after us.

Jan. 5, 1944.  We're having a tough time of it now.  Inspection is tomorrow and of course it means a lot of work.  Hope I can borrow a razor.  It was dumb of me not to check those blades before I left Denver.

Guess I didn't tell you about the trip out.  We had a lot of fun.  We were on the one car all the way to Los Angeles, then we transferred to a streamliner.  The Shore Patrol took charge of us and from there on we went and did what they wanted us to do, and not what we wanted to do.  You can have the Great Painted Desert; I don't want it.  There is some pretty country though.  I saw orange trees and apricot trees full of fruit; green grass and blooming flowers.  When they stopped the train, it was at such short intervals there wasn't time to write and find a mail box.  We thought we left a man in a little town in New Mexico.  He took a chance and just caught the end of the train as it went past.  He had to come the full length of the train to our car, and there were 18 cars at the time.

We had a good time with my harmonica after they found out I had it.  Too bad I had to send it home.  Maybe I can have it again later.

Don't try to follow me.  San Diego is more crowded than I thought a town could be.  A Marine Sgt. [Sergeant] met us at the station and put us on a bus with a lady driver.  She let us know how they drive in California.  If I had done some of the things with the school bus in Denver that she did with this thing, I'd have been thrown into the clink.

When we arrived at the base, I was sorry I was here, and how.  I've never in my life gone through such rough stuff.  Out here no one asks you to do anything and they don't say please.  When they give commands, they can be heard all the way across the base.

By the way, my rifle is a Gerand U.S. Cal. 30 M1 semi-automatic.

Putting up the flag here is quite impressive.  The Marine Band plays and the entire base halts and salutes.  Even cars and trucks stop.

Jan. 8, 1944.  I'll sure be glad when we get out of boot camp. Don't take that wrong.  I like it fine now even if it is a lot of hard work.  I thought I had done some hard work in my life, but I didn't even know what it was.  If and when I get back on the job, I will never again grumble.

Fifty per cent of us are supposed to make Pfc. (Private First Class) at the end of boot camp.  Hope I make it.  The only thing we all want now is for boot camp to be over with, Pfc. or no Pfc.

It sure looks funny to move a rifle at arm's length from me.  Each man has it hanging from his sack right beside him.  The firing pen has been removed and we have no ammunition.  The idea is to get us acquainted with it.

By the way, I signed up for $6.25 to be taken out of my check for bonds.  I didn't have any choice.  Didn't even know what I had signed until I was told.  I have signed a lot of papers without being allowed to read them.  They just line us up and tell us to sign on the dotted line.  But I don't think we have to worry about it.  Most of those I signed that I don't know about, I believe are for the supplies I was issued.

I hear we are to get some platoon pictures made tomorrow for the records.  Hope we get at least one of them to send home.  Don't think we will though.

Jan. 10, 1944.  If my papa had to sit on the side of his bed, or sack, as we call it here, and expect to be called out at any minute and have to chuck everything into a sea bag and get into the ranks in nothing flat, he wouldn't write very good either.  They don't give us notice when we are to be called out.  Sometimes they will tell us to stand by.  That may mean they will call us out in one minute or it may be one hour.  We have been standing by for more than 15 minutes now.  We can't leave anything out of the sea bag, and it has to be on the shelf near the ceiling.

I think of my little girls every now and then in the ranks and miss a command.  The D.I. then, in a very nice voice, as loud as he can shout, "You'll have to forget your family for a while. Remember, I'd like to go home, too."  We all get it like that.  We had bayonet drill today.  If I have to get it at all, I hope I get shot.

A fellow from Texas is in the hut here now, but is on his way home. He's a vet now. He came in the same day the rest of us did. He will get, so he says, $30 per month the rest of his life. He knocked a knee out of joint while marching. He told us that nine out of ten fellows that are in the sick bay got there because of the obstacle course. That's the one I told you I went over. It was the toughest thing I ever hope to encounter.

Jan. 13, 1944. We've had a hell of a time. I'm so tired I don't know which way to turn. I'm having a terrible time without razor blades. I can't get single-edge blades to fit my razor.

I saw my first ship today from a distance. I found out we are living right on the shore of a bay. I had thought I heard fog horns at night. I saw at least a dozen ships all at one time. They weren't more than eight blocks away. They were pretty good size.

Have a picture of the whole gang to send if I ever get to the post office to mail it. We had a parade today. General inspection tomorrow.

Jan. 14, 1944. Thanks so much for everything. It is sure swell. Just got the laundry bag, knife, sewing kit, and razor blades. Oh, yes, razor blades. I was never so glad to receive anything in my life. Have passed all inspections so far and there have been plenty.

I sure thought I and a lot of other fellows were going to land in sick bay this afternoon. They gave us some more shots in the left arm and it was hurting and making us all pretty sick and it still hurts. Then this Cpl. [corporal] took us out and made us run the commando course. I just made it the first time and I thought my lungs would burst. My left arm felt like it would drop off. Well, we didn't run it right. So we went the second time. Some of us wanted to kill us a Cpl.

We've been told to stand by to go out at 1845. Don't know what we'll do, but we would like to go to bed. We only got five and a half hours of sleep last night. Oh, well, I better stop that kind of stuff or I will have you feeling sorry for me. You know I'll be all right though. If I wasn't, I wouldn't be writing this letter.

Went to church last Sunday and think I will get to go again in the morning. It isn't what I'm used to, but it's quite impressive just the same.

We had a fire demonstration, almost the same thing I got in air raid training.

I passed the swimming qualifications--50 yards. I went to the end of the pool with the beginners and a guard came over (this was the third time I had been in) and tapped me on the shoulder and told me to get back to the other end of the pool. I told him I couldn't swim. He told me I was a liar. He took me down and shoved me off into ten feet of water and told me to swim 50 yards. I don't get to go swimming again in boot camp. Oh, well, I've got enough to do anyway.

Jan. 16, 1944. Sunday. We were each allowed to by 10¢ worth of candy the other day. I fondled the stuff like a little boy. I wasn't the only one, either. Sixty men, each hanging on to 10¢ worth of candy like our lives depended on it. Don't feel sorry for us--we'll live. A fellow in a foxhole can't have everything he wants either.

We went through the gas chamber last Friday. It wasn't as bad as I thought it would be. It looks like we are going to the rifle range next Saturday for three weeks. They say that is plenty tough, too. Each man is supposed to fire about 300 rounds of ammunition. It seems there are various ratings that can be acquired out there too. Expert rifleman get $5 a month for one year. Sharpshooter gets $3 a month for one year.

Jan. 16, 1944. I'm having fun with the work now. I make a lot of mistakes, but so does everyone else. I'm getting along with the manual of arms now. I made a mistake the other morning, though. The D. I. didn't say a word, just gave me a dirty look. He said plenty this morning when I let my mind wander and missed a command: "To the rear, march." I kept on straight ahead. I messed up the ranks and I don't mean maybe.

Jan. 19, 1944. It's been three weeks now since we arrived here. It doesn't seem that long. But when I go back over everything we have gone through, I wonder how we could do it in three weeks.

These Texans are nuts. They are looking for candy and they know there isn't any around. These rats are telling me to ask you for candy and cookies. But you would have to send so much for it to go around. The fellows that have received stuff just got a taste of it and that's all.

I haven't gotten a paycheck either and don't know when I'm supposed to get one. It looks like I might need about $5. I hate to ask for it. If you don't get your check in another few days, I'll see what I can find out. I'll get bawled out, but we get bawled out about everything. I'm getting so used to it I laugh at them, then get it in the neck for laughing. Oh well, I'm getting along pretty well anyway. It appears I've passed everything so far except the bayonet course. I just don't seem to be able to swing my body and arms the right way at the right time.

Guess I haven't told you about the D.I. (drill instructor).

Each platoon has a D.I., and the D.I. has two assistants. When I speak of the D.I. it means any one of the three. The D.I. is Lord and Master of the platoon. We are forced to say "Sir" to him every time it's necessary to speak to him. The Cpl. in the picture is the D.I. No one likes him. Some have declared their intention to murder him if they should go overseas together. I don't like the guy, but I haven't reached the murder stage yet.

Jan. 21, 1944. We're getting ready to go to the range tomorrow. We're planning to get up at 5 A.M. so we will have more time. Hope we make it. We're having a lotta fun putting everything we own in our sea bags--everything from soap and shoes to a #10 galvanized bucket. We don't want to leave the buckets behind. We use them for everything from fire buckets to wash tubs. All our personal effects have to go in the sea bag, then we lock it. We'll carry our rifles and packs. More fun.

Jan. 23, 1944. We're up at the rifle range now. It's very damp up here, but it isn't hurting like it did down at the base. They tell us it's going to be plenty tough here. I don't like the arrangement, but then the D.I. told us they used to bring up just one platoon at a time. This week 17 moved up and there were several already here.

Jan. 24, 1944. It's raining again here. The wind is blowing hard. However, rain or shine the Marine Corps keeps on the go. We were shown how to hold our rifles for firing in the prone and sitting positions today. We all thought they were going to break our arms. No other service in the world gets this same training, we're told, and I'm wondering why. I thought the rifle was going to twist right around me. I'm plenty stiff, too. In the sitting position the instructor sat right down on my back to put me in the position I should be in. I thought that was the end of me. I wasn't the only one. I think at that I came out better than some of the fellows did. I might add this all took place all day today and it rained and the wind blew all the time.

I received the needles in the letter; there were also some in the bottom of the sewing kit. I'm making good use of them, sewing pads on my elbows and shoulder where the rifle rests.

We saw a movie Sunday night. I almost missed it. We were supposed to have our pads sewn on in order to get to go. I didn't have mine on, along with some other guys. So when the D.I. and the others had left, I and another guy put on our hats and followed. Don't ask me why I did it. I don't know myself. Anyway, when we got to the theater (open air), we found we couldn't get in unless we were with a platoon and of course ours was already in. So what do we do? We back up and get on the tail-end of another platoon and walk in. My heart went thump-thump when the D.I. looked us over but said nothing.

Oh, well, life is so dull without my wife. I had a dream about my wife last night. It didn't end because some dope woke me up to see what time it was. We don't have a bugle out here, but we're expected to get up at 5 A.M. anyway. I never will forgive that guy.

It's started hailing--excuse please--it's quit hailing and is raining very hard. I wouldn't trade Colorado for a hundred states like California. You can throw Texas in too. Of course you understand I have three great interests in Colorado.

Jan. 26, 1944. We're doing what they call snapping-in. We'll get almost three weeks of it before firing for record. Every time I go through with it, I think my left arm is going to break off, but it doesn't. We also fired the .30 cal. carbine. I have never seen one before. It weighs just five and a half lbs. I made seven hits out of 12. This afternoon we fired a .22 caliber rifle. I think I did pretty good at that.

The Navy is brought in here to fire for the record. They get just one day for snapping-in where we get almost three weeks.

The rifle firing is rather interesting, but nothing funny. Everything is business. That was one time I couldn't let my mind wander. I think I can truly say I'm enjoying this more every day.

One person out of each squad is supposed to take part in a contest tonight: take down and put back the M1 rifle -- blind-folded. I can do pretty good but not blind-folded.

Jan. 30, 1944. We were on guard duty for the first time since coming to the range. It was exciting. That four hours went the fastest of any four in my whole life. I had one fire and one fight. The officer of the day stopped and I had to know answers. I made it all right, but I was slow, too slow.

The fire was in one of the huts on the "E" range. Oil heater caught fire. We are sure lucky living where we do. Those fellows are living, if you want to call it that, in a terrible mess.

I was sure glad to get the $5. I was hanging on to my last dollar. I hope it doesn't run you short. I don't know when we are supposed to get paid. Some say the last week of our boot training. We were told we wouldn't need any money, but we're finding out differently.

We fired the .30 cal. carbine for record. I did terrible on

the slow fire. I got the red flag (Maggie's drawers) on almost all shots. [Indicates a miss.] When it came to rapid fire I got six bull's eyes and four 4's. The next ring around the bull's eye is the 4 ring. This is becoming more interesting all the time. There's more work all the time too. It seems some of us have to change our pants again. I just got through taking up my pants' legs one-half inch; now I have to let them out one-half inch. I think I'll crawl off into a corner and pull out the hair I don't have.

Jan. 31, 1944. I fired the .22 again today. The rifle coach almost covered the shots with a dime. I got bawled out when he didn't. That was in the prone position at 25 feet. The other positions were about the same as before. The coach couldn't have covered those with a dollar. He gave me a real cussing.

We were given just 50 minutes to take a shower, wash clothes (underwear, socks and towel), and clean our rifles. I made it and polished my shoes on top of it. Can you imagine me moving that fast?

So it's snowing in Denver, and it's cold, too. It's been nice here the past couple of days. Time for some more liquid. I'm not in any desert. I'm in hilly country with a rifle range behind every hill. They even issued us another blanket. We have three now and two of those are doubled on our bunks. We are about 15 miles from the base, between San Diego and Los Angeles.

So you've heard about the mustering out pay? I've heard a lot of the fellows talking about it here. It might be of interest for you to know not one of them is in favor of a mustering out pay at all.

They aren't giving us all we can eat here. We always leave the mess hall hungry. Nothing we can do or say can get us any more. But it's nothing to worry about. There happens to be a reason for it. If we ate all we wanted, we wouldn't in this world be able to get into the positions we do somehow get into.

My dress uniform here is brown field shoes, green dress pants, khaki field shirt, field scarf (or tie), combat jacket and barracks cap (green). Combat jacket is almost khaki, a little light though. I was wearing everything but the jacket in the picture if you can tell anything about it. You can see the other fellows. We were all dressed alike. I will receive the full uniform like we saw in Denver at the end of boot camp. The blue dress uniform isn't issued at present. They can be gotten by spending $85. I don't think I'm interested. The blue dress is too hard to take care of anyway.

We don't work in the green uniform. We wear it when on guard duty, as messengers, in offices and when going to church or for inspections, etc. We wear them only when ordered to. As a matter of fact, we don't do anything without orders. We take showers, shave, wash our clothes, polish our shoes, go to chow, air our bedding, go to bed at night, change our clothes, etc., all under orders. We don't do anything until we get the order to do so, then we do it on the double. In other words, faster than it's possible to do so. We can't even go to the post office without permission, a matter of ten minutes there and back. When permission is given, the entire platoon marches in quick time. I'm getting used to it now, though. It won't be that way after boot camp--I hope.

It seems some of the fellows are to go across as soon as they finish boot camp. They go into training on some of the islands like Hawaii, etc. Some of them have been engineers. I might be going--I don't know. If I do go, it might be a month or more before you hear from me. Don't worry--they won't send me to the front until I'm ready for it, and I have a long way to go. I've known they have an engineering station in Hawaii, but was afraid I'd worry you. We all know I will go sooner or later.

Feb. 1, 1944. My watch is running again. The second hand is missing, but it gets us up on time. We can't hear the bugle here. Some mornings a bugler drives around in a jeep and blows his brains out.

Feb. 4, 1944. The sun is shining through the door on me now. It comes up in the north here. Yep, you guessed it--I haven't gotten my directions straight since I've been here.

Bought a pint of ice cream the other night. It was sure good. We weren't supposed to have it, but we got by with it. I think the D.I. knew about it.

Feb. 6, 1944. We fired our M1 rifles yesterday for the first time. What a hand full of boom. The first time I fired it, I thought the whole earth had blown up in front of me. The coach seemed to think I did all right. I'm not sure. I flinch when the other rifles go off beside me. There are only a hundred going off all at once, all on one range. There are several ranges close by. Heaven help the fellow that gets in the wrong place. If he doesn't get killed, he wishes he had; these coaches don't mess around with it at all. We were given 30 seconds to get off eight shots in rapid fire. There was no limit on time in slow fire. I got all my shots on the target, but that's all I can say for it.

I met a fellow who is on mess duty here that rode the school bus when I drove it. I didn't know him but he knew me.

He's been out of boot camp a week.

It appears I'm up for Pfc. It seems I've passed everything so far except for one item: I'm not one of the fellows. I don't shoot the bull enough. I manage to keep pretty much to myself. Therefore, I show no signs of leadership. I was given a lecture the other night long after everyone else was in bed. I've been aware for some time I need to break away from the shell I'm in. According to them, I've got to express myself and shoot the bull with the rest of the gang. I've made up my mind to do it. Don't believe I can learn to cuss like these fellows do though. Don't believe they're referring to that altogether, though. We're up against a dirty enemy and we have to learn how to cope with it.

Feb. 8, 1944. The big subject of the day now is firing for record next Thursday. We are all going to fire for expert and hope we make marksman. If I don't qualify I'm going to be pretty mad at myself. I'll probably stay a private during the whole time I'm in here, too. We fired pre-record today. I fired 281 out of a possible 340. That's marksman, because 268 or above makes marksman; 291 makes sharpshooter; 306 or above is expert. One fellow who was in the Marines before fired 321. Eight didn't qualify at all. What we make next Thursday is what counts.

Most of the fellows have gone to the show. I felt too tired to go and besides, it's raining. It's an outdoor theater. It's raining pretty heavy right now. Our hut is leaking. I'm glad it isn't over my bunk.

Feb. 11, 1944. I'm in pretty much of a hurry. We go back to the base in the morning. I'm sorry I can't find more time to write. I made rifle expert. I scored 308 out of a possible 340. There were eight of us made expert in this platoon. Only four of the Texans made expert. We're throwing the mud at them now. I'm supposed to get an extra $5 per month on my check now for a year. The highest score made was 318. There were two in our platoon that didn't qualify on the range. They tell me I get a medal, but I have to pay for it.

I found out about the pay. They took out the allotment for Jan. and Feb. plus three months for insurance. I didn't receive anything again when they paid off last night. Only a few did get anything. They were single fellows.

We're enjoying the candy and nuts. The raisins were going over real big until I ditched them. The only trouble is I have to pack about half of it to move to the base. It seems we can go to bed now, and I think I'll do it. It's 9:50 and we are to get up at 0430.

Feb. 15, 1944.  We have drawn the rest of our uniform.  I look pretty nice.  We haven't gotten the barracks cap, and I don't think we will.  We also got some khaki for summer wear.  We slept with our dog tags for the first time last night.  The D.I. told us we would find out Friday where we go.  Several of the fellows have had interviews on cooking, radar, air corps, etc.

Platoon 1204 is in the dog house now.  Some of the boys got caught throwing craps.  The whole platoon is getting it in the neck.  Gambling is a court martial offense.  I wasn't in on it. That's something I can't go for.

Training postcard:  cargo nets

We had a good time with the package the folks sent.  The D.I. thought he saw a bottle of whiskey and grabbed the package away from me.  I laughed and laughed when he pulled out a jar of sweet pickles.  I thought he was going to throw me over the fence.  He ordered me to get rid of it at chow last night which I did.  We can't have anything with glass.  Took several pickles for myself and passed it down the table.  It didn't get very far before it was empty.  One of the fellows grabbed the jar and held it aloft. That's the way we get bowls and pitchers refilled.  The messman came along, looked at the jar, read the label, then shouted, "Where the hell did that come from?"  We all had a lot of fun out of it.

Feb. 13, 1944.  We've been told we can go to the show at the base theater if we have our gear in shape.  I didn't want to go anyway.  I had to take time out and get these guys some raisins. They sure are good.  They're arguing now whether or not they're rationed.

It's hard to know where I'm going from here.  There's a lot of rumors going around, but none that I want to believe.  Then the time comes we are given orders and then we do our best to carry them out.

I have hopes of calling you on the 20th [wedding anniversary]; but I might be any place:  train, truck, bus, or boat.

We're back at the base.  Some of the fellows have gone to church.  Something happened to my watch.  I thought I had plenty of time, but they left before I could get ready.  My watch was running; I don't know what happened.

The guys here are talking over the orders and rules.  We expect a test on the whole Red Book sometime this week.  The Red Book is our handbook.  The test isn't going to be easy.  Some of the fellows have already taken tests for radar, radio, typing, etc. These were special tests they were called in for.  I've taken a lot of tests, but of course I don't know how I came out on them.

Last night we were all talking about the changes that had taken place in each of us since we have arrived here.  We have all changed.  We couldn't help but change.

Training postcard:  establishing a beach head

Feb. 20, 1944.  From:  Pfc. Fred T. Klemm, 13-b-11 56th Rep. H.S. Co. Engineer Battalion, T.C. Camp Pendleton, Oceanside, Calif.  I couldn't get permission to call you, so I got up early and took the chance a guard wouldn't stop me.  I made the call and then crawled back into bed.  I didn't sleep though.  I've let them give me all the work they could shove at me this morning; I don't want too much time to think.

I have some more sewing to do:  my stripes, of course. The Pfc. (on the address) means I made it.  13-B-11 is the barracks number.  56th Rep is 56th Replacement.  The other is Engineer Battalion, Training Center.

I've been busy, and how.  Nothing hard, but plenty to do. They tell me this is really tough.  We have been told not to say too much about what we're doing, so you know what to expect.  I know for sure we'll be here for five weeks and possibly 13.  This is called basic training.  Some of it is going to be plenty tough, like jumping off a 35-foot tower and swimming 200 yards.  Don't worry--of course I can't do it now, but I will.

Camp Pendleton is about 17 miles from Oceanside and about 50 miles from the San Diego Marine Base.

It's tough coming into a new place and learning all the rules.  I might add I'm scared silly.  We have a Lt. [Lieutenant] as a platoon leader.  He seems nice.  I hope I don't mess things up. We don't get much liberty even yet.  I haven't got it straight just what we do get.  I know there won't be a furlough for some time.

There were three from the boot camp platoon that came into the engineers.  They really gave us an inspection when we left the base.  There were 27 of us that got Pfc.  I was glad to get it.  If I can go on up now I'll be all right.

Feb. 22, 1944.  They're keeping us plenty busy.  Classes day and night.  What with keeping gear clean and all, we have all we can take care of.  Some studying to do too.

The Lt. tells us we will be here 14 weeks.  Afterward we go to Camp Elliott.  We will be there maybe a day, a week, a month.  The Lt. and the whole group except some that won't make the grade will go together.

I don't write down everything I know.  Even so, keep shut. One fellow got six years hard labor because his dad let something slip.

I don't get to write very often.  I even hang on to your

letters lots of times for hours before I get to open them. It was that way in boot camp and it will be worse here. The other fellows are in the same fix. We all like to receive letters though.

Feb. 24, 1944. It quit raining about 4 P.M. or 1600. We're all pretty happy about it. There isn't much I can tell you except I'm doing all right at present. I'm seeing a lot of film, and hearing a lot of lectures, and I know how to fire the light machine gun now. I saw the official film on the bombing of Pearl Harbor. I never knew the half of it before.

My bunk is almost in the door of the squad room. Worse luck. Every officer that looks in sees mine first. And, too, each time an officer comes in, the first guy that sees him shouts "Attention!" Oh, well. I'll be running you nuts when I get home. I'll be making up the bed as soon as I hit the deck in the mornings, I'll be wiping off the bulkhead, etc. Oh, well, in a way it's a lot of fun.

We go to class at 1830 and it's now 1820 so I better be moving along. They're keeping me on my toes. Maybe that's what I've been needing all along.

Class is over and I have just cleaned my rifle. We're now waiting for the Officer of the Day (O.D.) to inspect our barracks. They asked for volunteers to clean up the classroom so I did. The Cpl. had a funny look on his face when he saw how clean it was. So I had to tell him what work I'd been doing.

Don't believe all the fishy tales you hear and don't repeat them. Scuttlebutt loses lives the same as truth. I could tell you a lot of tales, and will someday, that are true, but you will find them hard to believe.

Feb. 27, 1944. Some of the fellows have returned from liberty and some of the stories they told were funny and some weren't. Two fellows hitch-hiked to San Diego. They were picked up by two lady Marines. They didn't notice until they had climbed into the back that they were 2nd Lts. They "Yes, Ma'med" their way all the way to San Diego.

It looks like we will have weekends pretty much to ourselves. The only thing I had to do was keep myself and my sack looking pretty. Wore my uniform to church this morning. I think I looked pretty good.

I understand some time during the next four or five weeks we are to make a landing from landing boats in the ocean. We will have blanks in our rifles. The fellows defending the shore will have machine guns with live ammunition. The machine guns are to be fired just a few inches above our heads. The Lt. doesn't think we can keep our butts down. It isn't our heads he's worried about. As for my part, I'm going to dig a tunnel under the barbed wire. Oh, yes, there's to be barbed wire which will be booby-trapped with explosives that are to explode a few feet from us. Every so often, the Lt. tells us, some T.N.T. will explode. It's easy to write about it now. I wonder what it'll be like afterward.

Of course no one is supposed to get hurt. If he keeps down, that is. They won't have to tell me twice. I'll tell you all about it when it's over. It's all part of our training to condition us for combat.

Some of the fellows jumped from what they called the 20-foot tower into water yesterday, but the guard on duty told me it was actually 30 feet. They didn't let me jump. It seems I can't swim yet. I'm not the only one, though.

Feb. 26, 1944. I'm having trouble with my swimming. We are supposed to swim without making a splash: in other words, quietly.

We were given three choices a little while ago for what we want to go into. I chose heavy equipment: tractors, bulldozers, etc. Second choice: demolition (use of T.N.T., etc.) Third choice: camouflage (hiding from the enemy). The Lt. says heavy equipment is the worst. I disagree. Anyway, so many men have to go into it. I can't see myself crawling up on a pill box and throwing dynamite into it, and I don't care much for this kind of art (camouflage).

We've been assigned platoons and squads. I had to move my bunk or sack into the other end of the squad room. At least I'm not right in the door now.

Feb. 28, 1944. The special delivery airmail doesn't get to me any faster than the regular mail.

I can't tell you much about the studies here at present. We went into what they call combat conditioning, where we all almost went to sick bay. One fellow had to have the care of the corpsman. They had corpsmen placed all over the place, so I guess they were expecting something. This afternoon they started us on demolition: how to handle dynamite and T.N.T. and a lot of other stuff. If I do what they expect us to do with that stuff and come out in one piece, I won't be afraid of anything.

The engineers are the infantry plus the building of roads, bridges, and anything else that happens their way. If you know anything about the infantry, you know that they are right in the front. The engineers, it has been said, often go beyond the front to do their work. On the way, of course, they may need to knock out some pill boxes and look for land mines.  We're supposed to be learning all about it.  That's the way it was done on many of the islands we have taken.  The engineers are either along with the infantry and know how to use all their weapons, or they're ahead of them clearing the way.  One officer said we were infantry first and engineers second.  We may have to work with a rifle in our hands.  The Marine paratroops and the Raiders have been disbanded and many are now a part of the engineers.  When I say I'm with fast company, I don't mean maybe.  Our instructors have all served overseas.

The reason it's taking so long to get Germany out of the way is (I'm told) because the Marines aren't taking care of them. When we get finished with the Japs, we'll go over and help the Army.  Okay, okay.  Anyway, remember the Marines are doing all the dirty work in the Pacific.  The Army takes over when the Marines have cleared the way.

Feb. 29, 1944.  I set off my first T.N.T. today.  What a bang.  The fuse was about 4 inches long on a half-pound block of T.N.T.  We would light it, then walk away.  It took about ten seconds to explode.

March 1, 1944.  The Sgt. of the Guard let me go down to the post office and get my package.  The $5 will hold me over plenty good. The pound of mixed nuts is already gone, and almost another pound of peanuts.  I'm smoking my pipe now.  One of the fellows here said that's the kind of wife he was going to marry.  I showed them the pictures and they almost blew off the roof when they saw the girls.  Most of the fellows are single.  Some have as many as five children.  They are very few, though.

March 5, 1944.  I passed the 100-yard test in swimming.  They let us use any stroke we wanted, so long as we didn't break the surface.  I used the dog paddle most of the time.  Next week I will go into a different class.  I will jump off the 15-foot tower, I hope.

I got wet the other night on guard duty.  I had a nice time cleaning up my greens.  While we were standing by for guard duty, I heard my first radio program since I left Denver.  It was a newscast. Navy bombers had hit Wake.  Don't know yet just how the raid came out.  We get papers every now and then.  I didn't find one today.

All our posts around here are challenging posts.  I didn't have one person come on my post, including the O.D.  We have to challenge him, too.  Some of the fellows had him come onto their post, and I guess from what they said, they did it all wrong and got bawled out.  One 2nd Lt. out on Post 6 decided he wanted to know just how good the guards were and started to horse around with a truck.  The guards on the post carry loaded rifles with orders to bring back a human if they bring back an empty shell. Well, this guard never even thought about his loaded rifle; he went to work with his bayonet. The O.D. came along just in time to save the Lieutenant.  More fun.

The duty non-commissioned officer for the weekend has been coming to me to find out what to do.  He gives an order, and the guys just tell him to go and stay put.  I turn around and tell them to carry out the order.  They give me a dirty look and mumble something and go do it.  Why?  I don't know.  I've been expecting someone to push my teeth down my throat but it hasn't happened yet.

I didn't go out this weekend because I was on standby. In other words, if something went wrong, regardless of what or where, those on standby are called out.  We are supposed to get liberty two weekends out of three.  We can leave at 11:00 A.M. on Saturday and are to be back by 6:00 Monday morning.

The fellows can't find a place to stay, however, unless they go home with some girl.  They call it "shacking up."  Some have their wives here who drive out and pick them up on Saturdays and bring them back early Monday morning.  If we come in after 6:00 we are charged with being absent without leave.  Every case has received a sentence.  Some got ten days on bread and water.  Some who came in only a few minutes late were given EPD, "extra police duty."  Some have been restricted with "no more liberty."

I'm not sure yet, but I think I have lost out on heavy equipment.  I talked myself blue in the face, too, besides running a bulldozer over a steep embankment, down through some brush and back up again just to show them I could do it.  Of course I have never been on one before and they knew it.  They left me without saying a word.  They could only take so many in there and it was filled up right away with fellows who did that kind of work before they came in the service.  I don't know where I will land. It sounds like I might land in the assault engineer company now. I hate to think about it, because to tell you the truth, it is just about the roughest thing there is.  It comes next to the infantry or I should say it is the infantry and the engineers together.  While these fellows are taking the specialist course, we will be learning a little bit about everything the Marine combat engineers do.  I think part of them carry the M1 and part the carbine or Ricing gun. The Ricing gun is something I haven't told you about, mostly because I don't know too much about it myself, but I do know it spits out bullets as long as you hold the trigger back. It's a rifle fired from the shoulder and is lighter than the M1. It's carried by the MPs (Military Police), or permanent guard.

March 13, 1944. I took leave and went into Oceanside yesterday. It's just another nice little town pretty well taken over by Marines. I felt funny walking down the street in uniform. Went into the USO. It was a flop. Went to a movie and saw "The Strange Death of Hitler." Was a pretty good show.

Eleanor Roosevelt was here a while back and went through the camp. She went into one of the mess halls and looked around. When they went into the galley, there was a mess Sgt., stripped to the waist, rolling out bread dough. He would pull it out, slam it down and hit it with his stomach and make it roll across the table. She watched him for a while and then they left. When she got ready to leave, the Col. [Colonel] asked her what she thought of the camp. She said she thought it was swell except she thought the mess Sgt. was a bit unsanitary. The Col. said, "Oh, no, you should see him when he rolls out donuts."

We started our camouflage training today. It's proving more interesting than I thought it would. They took some of the fellows out and fixed them up and the rest of us went out to see if we could find them. I thought, well, I have pretty good eyes, and they would have to be hidden pretty well to keep me from seeing them. That's where I was fooled. I walked within three feet of one and didn't see him. The interesting part about it was that he was in plain sight and I had looked right at him. He was sitting in front of a bush. They had him fixed so that he would blend right in with the background. They had 13 of them hidden and I didn't even find one of them. They would let us go on by them and then fire at us or throw hand grenades at us. Blanks, of course. If they really had been Japs I'm afraid we would all have been wiped off the map. It was most interesting.

March 15, 1944. I don't know what to say, sweetheart. I was surprised as well as pleased: the package was something out of the next world. The fellows went wild, to say nothing of the way I felt. The fellows said such wonderful things. Some of them were even trying to do my work for me. Some of them are promising to show me around when I get ready to go to L.A. How did you know I couldn't find the medal? I was surprised. One of the fellows was looking at the gloves when he remarked there was something in one of them. I said it must be the fountain pen. He said "no" and pulled out the medal. We all just sat and stared at it. Thanks a lot! I can get some pictures made now the next time

I get into town.

I'm writing in our new recreation room. I didn't even know it was here until I blundered into it by mistake. It just happened I was wearing the right uniform. It's as large as the one end of the barracks I'm living in and has several tables, three radios, and a phonograph. There are magazines and books all over the place. We live on the second floor and it's on the first. There's a classroom on the other end of the barracks.

Yesterday I was all painted up in green and brown paint. We had flowers, limbs, leaves and shrubs stuck all over us. We had a sham battle. It was a lot of fun except I almost got sick. We had to crawl through shrubs, trees and rocks, over a hill and down across a creek. It had rained all night the night before. I feel okay now. I don't think even you would have known me the way I was fixed up. Our side won the sham battle. We were the invaders. As I crawled, I went right by two fellows and didn't see them and they didn't see me. I went within five feet of both of them. The were sitting still, watching for us to come through and of course, we were moving.

March 19, 1944. It was good to hear the voices of my favorite girls. All three sounded just swell. While I think of it, this will be the last letter I will be able to write or receive for about ten days. Don't worry about me.

The package came through with grand colors. I didn't get to taste the chocolate cake. I had already gone to bed when the Lt. sent the Cpl. in for it. He and another officer ate it all. The following morning, he went through the barracks and took down, or rather had the Cpl. take down, all the names he called off. Mine was one of them. The crust of him. Of course, I don't think he connected me at the time with the cake. It wouldn't have made any difference anyway because I had it coming. I left my poncho out on my sack. I ended up with five hours EPD. More fun. I haven't talked to him since. I was going to ask him if the cake made him sick. The Cpl. told me that they liked it very much.

I'm still trying to get the rest of the package eaten up before we leave. The cheese and crackers are all I have left. I ditched most of it after what happened. I'm afraid the cheese won't keep until I return. So I think after inspection, I'll let the fellows in on it. I let them in on the other cake. They all want more of it. There have been a dozen or so that have asked for your address so they can thank you themselves. I don't know if they will do it or not. They were, I'm sure, sincere in what they told me, which was very nice. They all, including the Cpl., come to me every now and then and ask if I have received another package from you.  Most of them know it when a package arrives, though.  The mail call is out in the open.  Very few packages are received.  Don't make them too large.  I can't put them any place.  I don't want any more EPD.

March 26, 1944.  I should have written sooner, but I was so tired on my return that I just laid myself down and went to sleep.

Our week of hard work, excitement and fun is over. Several fellows got hurt, but none seriously.  About the worst was a sprained ankle.  No, nobody got shot.

The infiltration course was about 200 yards long.  There were three trenches.  We started out from one of them and rested, or were supposed to if we wanted to, in the one in the middle. Then in the last one, we fixed bayonets and got up and ran to a dummy and stuck it in to finish the course.  In between the trenches there were sand bags, barbed wire, shrubs, little mounds, to say nothing of the land mines, booby traps, and other explosives that were set off by electricity from a safe place. There was irritant smoke, too.  Three machine guns fired .30 cal. rounds over our heads about 18 to 30 inches.  Every fifth round was a tracer so we could see real bullets were passing over us.  I looked up just once and saw the grass being clipped off of a mound right beside me.  We wore packs and carried our rifles. We had to turn over on our backs to get through the barbed wire we held up with our rifles.  Booby traps were attached to the barbed wire so all we had to do was move the wire and it would set off some explosives.

There were shell holes all over which they told us we could crawl into if we felt we needed to rest.  There was just one thing wrong with that: they didn't tell us they had land mines and booby traps in there, too.  There were trails all through the course which we could follow until we were stopped by sand bags.  All along these trails were land mines and booby traps.  I was in the first relay of 20 men to go through.  By the time the other relays came through, the land mines were pretty well all set off.  Once I saw some brush in front of me and started to move it out of my way when I noticed a little glint of light on wire.  I left it lay and crawled over it.  The fellow just behind me decided he didn't want to go over it, so he pulled it out of his way.  My legs went up in the air and my nose went in the dirt.  After I had left the second trench, I thought I was going pretty good.  I could see the fellow at the loud speaker and I could see the last trench just a few feet away and I was doing my best to get there in a hurry.  I forgot, of course, that the fellow on the loud speaker could see me too. Every time one of us got our butts a little too high, he would yell over that speaker at us and at the same time the machine guns would concentrate on the fellow with his butt high. I didn't have to be yelled at for that but just as I felt that I had made it, the earth raised up in front of me and covered me with dirt. My ears were whining at me two hours. I ducked, of course, and when I tried to go forward again, I couldn't, so I looked to see what was stopping me. Yes, it had been T.N.T. that went off about a foot in front of me. I could see the wires that led off to a fellow beside the man with the loud speaker. The hole it made was a good three feet in diameter and about a foot-and-a-half deep. I could hear the fellows laughing on the loud speaker. I looked up at them and felt like I wanted a loaded rifle. I crawled around it though and finished the course in what I believe was about 45 minutes. After it was all over, I started shaking. Maybe I shouldn't tell you all this, but there is no danger so long as we do as we are told.

I can now tell you I've been on the ocean twice. I can also say I have tasted ocean water. Yes, you guess it, but I wasn't the only one who fell. But my poor rifle. I still haven't gotten all the rust out of it. It went all the way to the bottom, with me hanging on to it, of course.

All and all it was a lot of fun. The first time we landed, we were already wet from water coming over the side. Then when we came into shore, we found that it was low tide and the boat grounded some distance from shore. I was expecting to get pretty wet, so I took a jump into the water and landed right in front of a breaker and down I went. That was when the rifle went all the way under. The second landing was made at dawn the following morning. The tide was high and the boat could come in closer, but the water was much rougher. When the landing ramp went down, I was completely dry. That was when I did do some cussing, because I saw more water ahead of me and, as before, I jumped. I took a flying leap at the water as if I didn't care if I did get wet. But when I landed, there wasn't any water there. I turned around in surprise and then I heard the Lt. who was leading yell. When I saw the large breaker hit the boat and knock it towards me, I didn't have to be told the second time to get out of there. I had run to the top of the sand bank when I fell and looked back to see the boat come broadside of the shore and the water hit my feet and then recede. A large number of the fellows were still in the boat. I don't think I ever heard a fellow yell quite as loud as that little fat 2nd Lt. did who was leading us. I never knew there were so many men in the Navy either, but they showed up then and it wasn't long until they had all the men off the boat and we were ordered to charge the country ahead and take charge of the highway and railroad which we did. After that, we drove the enemy back some 20 miles into the hills.  More fun. We got wetter in the tall grass than we did making the landing that second morning.

We spent the next three days in a blind canyon.  I might add that if you didn't know it, you wouldn't know that there were 150 men camped down there.  There were no signs of it at all. The whole thing was to simulate being on the front lines.  We carried our rifles and wore our steel helmets at all times.  When I say at all times, I mean just that.  We slept with our clothes on and our rifles in bed with us so that we were ready for anything that came. I had been in bed about an hour that first night when the guard was attacked.  I was told about it the next morning. Yes, you guessed it:  I was one of two men that slept through it all. Everybody was called out and everybody went except for two men.  I do remember raising up and looking out of the tent and seeing that it was very dark, thought that the Lt. would take of everything, and went back to the pillow that wasn't there.  We two felt rather funny when we were the only ones to fall out in the morning without bruises and cuts and scratches all over us.  Torn clothes could be seen every place.  The whole thing was done of course to show us just what could happen if we were in enemy territory.  There was one guard that was on the alert.  Four men attacked him and he grounded them all.  Two guards had their rifles taken away from them and they were tied and gagged.  I held down one of those posts Friday night from midnight until 2 A.M. It was so dark I couldn't see my hand in front of me. Nothing happened, though.

We were up again at 3 A.M. and we attacked a hill a few miles away that was defended by two platoons, along with barbed wire and all the stuff that goes with it.  When that was over, the score keepers called it a draw.  After that, we got all our stuff together and marched five and a half miles in 55 minutes.  We were all pretty glad to get back to our barracks.

I was in the Lt.'s office making up his bed when I heard him make the statement that there were two or three fellows in the outfit that hadn't given him enough trouble for him to know their names.  I looked around at him and he looked at me and I said that I'd bet him he didn't know my name.  He said no, he didn't.  I told him it was my wife who had made the cake.  He said he knew that and it was damn good chocolate cake, too.  "But you haven't caused me enough trouble for me to know your name." Me, I just said maybe I should start causing you some trouble, and let it go at that.  He just laughed and I never did tell him my name.

A Cpl. tells me I'm in the assault engineers.  Haven't

received the official notice yet, though. They were going to move us to another barracks but it seems there wasn't room enough there. It's all right with me. Don't worry about me being in the assault engineers. I talked with a fellow who is in there and it doesn't sound so bad to me.

March 28, 1944. I'm on guard duty. Supernumerary this time. Standing by to run errands for the Officer of the Day, and answer the phone in the Sgt. of the Guard office. Don't think I'll get wet tonight. At first, they assigned me to post 6A and then took me off of it. The guard there carries a loaded rifle. It's out on the boondocks where the Raiders almost killed a guard about a year ago. By the way, the assault engineers, we are told, are taking the place of the Raiders. Yes, that's what I'm in. We're supposed to learn how to assault the enemy positions, knock out pill boxes and machine gun nests. We will learn how to use the flame thrower, to fire the bazooka or rocket launcher, and a lot of other stuff. After we have taken the position, we are supposed to know how to build up our own defenses, like roads, bridges, pill boxes, etc. Don't worry, it won't be so bad. Our instructors are fellows who already seen action.

The Lt. knows my name now, and I didn't tell him, either. It seems we are getting along pretty good.

It doesn't seem I've been in the service three months. It's hard to believe. We heard over the radio they're going to have to draft fathers. That's too bad. I don't know what us childless fellows will do with them. Two-thirds of the men in our company are married and have from one to five children.

Change of address: Pfc. Fred T. Klemm (56), Engineer Battalion, T.C., Camp Pendleton, Oceanside, Calif.

March 29, 1944. I went over to sign the payroll tonight and found my name wasn't even on the books. Only one out of every ten in our group found his name there. We have been transferred to another company and the books got messed up. It just means we wait another month for our pay. Lt. Boyd and Sgt. Munger were pretty upset about it. They will both get paid; but they seem to think we should get some too. Sgt. Munger was shoving a lot of dirty words at some of the officers. It's the married men getting it in the necks again. It seems there just isn't anything left after they take out the allotment, bonds, insurance, etc.

While I was supernumerary on the guard yesterday, Sgt. Moody was killed while instructing a class how to make hand grenades out of one-half pound. T.N.T. blocks. He thought the fuse hadn't lighted.  He went to pick it up and it exploded.  Five members of the class were hurt.  All were in my company.  Some of the men are taking up a collection for Sgt. Moody's baby due in a week.

Such is life:  here today, gone tomorrow.

I'm pretty tired tonight.  I sawed logs this morning and dug post holes this afternoon.

April 2, 1944.  They caught up with me.  I'm on mess duty for the next 30 days.  I've been plenty busy since Friday morning.  The 52nd Rep. has left.  A lot of them were on mess duty.  Many Marines are moving in here.  "Little Tokyo" is being built to make room.  I helped break the ground for that.  It seems the engineers will be moving into that.  The 5th division is taking over the 13 area.  I've known for several days I won't be in the 5th division.  They tell us, the 17 who went on mess duty, that we won't lose our place in the 56th Rep.

At first there were only the 17 of us on mess duty.  Then 27 more came in from boot camp and were put on mess duty.  I'm running the dish washer.  It's all right except I have to put in some long hours.  I thought I had passed some tough inspections until I passed the one Saturday morning on mess duty.  The Col. himself looked us over.

They keep shoving in more men.  Sunday mornings for breakfast they have been feeding about 150 men.  This morning we served more than 600.  Yesterday we were called out of our bunks at 4:30 A.M.  When we finished the day, it was 7:55 P.M.  We had two hours off during that time.  One nice thing about it: we eat plenty.  Yes, I think I shall gain some more weight.

April 5, 1944.  We moved from barracks 13-B-11 to 13-B-6, the engineer company barracks.  I notice the First Sgt. who is standing near me now has five hash marks on this sleeve.  Each hash mark means four years in service.

There are 14 of us on mess duty now.  Twelve of us have our sacks in the same squad room with a bunch of NCOs [non-commissioned officers].  You can see we are on the spot right there.  We're waked up by the guard a 5 A.M.  We get to the mess hall at 5:30 A.M.  I got off one hour this afternoon.  I stood by this morning while the five fellows working with me took off two hours.  We take turns standing by.  I really got it, too.  Of course everything has to happen at the wrong time. First, they brought in a lot of work.  Then the darn washer stopped up and I, you know me, I crawled inside and took care of it.  Yeah, I know.  At first I didn't think I could take 30 days of it, but I'm getting used to it now.  I'm not as tired as I was at first.

April 9, 1944.  I got my first liberty in three weeks.  I'm still on mess duty.  I found suddenly Friday night through a lot of harsh words, I'm supposed to be in charge of the scullery (dishwasher) and didn't know it.  I know it now.  I have five men under me.  It seems I'm in hot water all the time.  So are the rest of the men.  Every time we turn around, we find we have done something wrong.

We 12 men are now in the 58th Rep.  We're sleeping in the same squad room with a large number of NCOs who are in the 54th Rep. and are waiting to be shipped out.  Most of them have already been overseas.  We 12 men get no orders until we find it is past time to obey them.  Of course you know what happens then.  We are under orders from both the C.O. (commanding officer) of the engineer company and also the C.O. of the mess hall.  Sometimes both issue orders at the same time.  With us, the mess hall has to come first.

We came in Saturday afternoon all ready to go on liberty and found the Col. had inspected the barracks after he had been over the mess hall and had dumped out somebody's locker box and found a lot of stuff that wasn't supposed to be there and restricted the entire barracks until everybody's box had been looked into.  Of course everyone had to be in the uniform of the day and there couldn't be anything to eat in the box.  Yes, I had the pound of raisins in there and some of the pies and nuts.  No place to put them so they would be out of sight.  I couldn't feed them to anybody because they were too full after having eaten what they had in their own boxes.  I had just five minutes to get ready.  I made it.  I still have the goodies.  I put the whole business in a G.I. can (trash can) near my bunk.  When he had looked at my box, I went back to the can, got my goodies, and neatly packed them back in my box.  Even the NCOs laughed at me.  They wouldn't tell.  They were a mad bunch of fellows.  As soon as the C.O. was out of the room, they changed into greens and were ready to go on liberty.  Then they received the order to fall out in khaki, under arms.  That's when I ducked out the back door followed by several other messmen.  We were just too tired.

Well, it looks like we aren't going to be paying any taxes this year.

I almost got into something else the other evening.  You know curiosity killed the cat.  One of the fellows who had been across with the Raiders was showing some of the fellows in the back of the room some jujitsu.  I went to see what was going on.  So, with my pipe in my mouth, I wandered back to the outside of the throng and I found that I was tall enough to look over the men who were there. Then suddenly I saw that it was a mistake to have wandered back there, but it was too late. "Now with a tall man, it is different," I heard the loud voice say. Of course I was a little surprised and too slow to see what is coming, so I suddenly found myself flying through the air. I no sooner came down than I heard a voice say, "And this is the way you stop a tall man when he comes at you with a swing." Of course I was already up and coming at him just like he expected me to do. So my pipe went one way while I went the other. I thought then and there that it was time for me to withdraw. Of course I didn't make it. I suddenly found myself with my feet in the air and my nose scraping the floor. Then my arm was twisted and I fell. While the voice explained the next move, I crawled out between the guy's legs, grabbed my pipe that I saw was about to set somebody's bunk on fire, said "Goodbye" and I went out the back door in a hurry. I wasn't hurt, but that guy knew too durn well what he was doing. Oh, well, these dopes have to have a laugh on somebody. It isn't always me.

April 11, 1944. I'm pretty busy. I have a couple of hours off this morning though. I don't know just when or where we will be moving, but from things that are taking place at present, it looks like it won't be long. It's possible, but not probable, that we will be sent east. That is, across to Europe. It's possible I'll be writing from some of the eastern states. I don't know.

It's cold in this darn place. They have some silly rule the windows have to stay open.

April 13, 1944. I'm still washing dishes. I signed the payroll the 12th. I will get $30 this time. We signed it a bit early for the married men. I don't know when we will get it. That should be enough to keep me going for awhile. I'm going to stick to taking care of my money until I get another pay, then what I have left over I can spend for some presents to send home.

April 16, 1944. A list of names is on the bulletin board: available for transfer. Mine is there.

April 26, 1944.  Pfc. Fred T. Klemm, Engineer Battalion, T.C. Camp Lejeune, No. Carolina.

If I don't know what it's like to ride a train, I'll never know. I thought for sure I'd be going west, but went east instead. I don't quite understand what we are doing here, but it seems we are to go through a special basic training course of four weeks. When we graduate from this, we are supposed to get some kind of promotions.  We are all wondering what it is all about.

This camp is very interesting.  The trip across the country, the people, things that happened to us, were all very interesting. Snowstorm in the Rockies, yes, in Colorado.  We didn't hit Denver. We were slated to, until I asked to be allowed to see you or at least call.  Then we turned off at Glenwood Springs and went to Pueblo.  We were held up by floods in Kansas and Missouri.  We're restricted to barracks at present.

April 27, 1944.  They're plenty strict about everything here.  As far as I'm concerned, it's nothing more than advanced boot camp. Double dose.  The barracks here are the best I've seen.  They are built of brick, have very good lighting and are steam heated.  The whole camp is like a big city with sidewalks, paved streets, lawns, trees and parks.  As soon as we have been interviewed and placed where they want us, we are to move again.  We haven't unpacked our sea bags.  The mess halls are quite different here. The tables are all set when we go in.  The officers eat in one end. The women reserves have a section where they eat. We eat out of china dishes instead of trays. We don't do our own washing here, either.  It is sent to the laundry (after we get settled).  It doesn't cost very much.

Most of the men who were already here have the impression we all just came out of boot camp.  There are some here with us who have spent as much as 18 months overseas. Most of them have been in the service longer than I have.

The feeling between north and south, and between the east and west can be seen very easily.  I believe I like No. Carolina as the country goes better than California.

The trip over was good, considering some of the things we had to go through.  We were restricted for two days before we left Camp Pendleton.  Most of us had the feeling we were going across.  Although the scuttlebutt told us New River, North Carolina, we didn't believe it.  The Captain in charge of the trip told us a few hours before we boarded the train that it was going to Camp Lejeune. Letters were slipped off the train and one telegram was sent. This fellow saw his family in Kansas City, but he got caught. I don't know what will happen to him, if anything. I had plenty of chances to slip letters off, but you know me, I always want to do the right thing if at all possible.

We boarded the train in Camp Pendleton at noon on Wednesday the 19th. We had supper in L.A. The train was a long one, and all Pullman cars, with more than 300 men and officers. We had guard duty during the entire trip, too. No civilians were allowed on without a pass and no Marines could get off the train. Two did in Salt Lake City, though, and we haven't seen them since. It was snowing in Salt Lake City and it was the first snow some of the men had seen. It was of course the first time I had seen the Great Salt Lake. When we arrived in Salt Lake City, I was sure we would be going through Denver. So, I asked and was told we would. Then I asked if I might be allowed to see you or at least call. I didn't get an answer. Several hours later, after we were in Colorado on our way to Grand Junction, I asked again and was told we wouldn't be stopping or if we did stop, nobody would get off. By that time, I was pretty well going nuts. I made up my mind to try to slip off a note to you. I was sure they would be watching me pretty close, though. They had roll call each time we started up again after a stop. One man who skipped in Salt Lake City was sitting in the train, wondering more or less out loud about his family when he looked out of the window and there stood his wife staring at him with an open mouth. She was on her way to California to see him.

After we left Glenwood Springs, it looked to me like we were going the wrong direction to be going to Denver. This was the first time I had my directions straight since I left Denver. I caught the conductor when he went through and he told me we would maybe go within a hundred miles of Denver. We were on our way to Pueblo. We were going through mountains now that were straight up on each side of the train. Once in awhile we hit a valley where we could see for quite a way. I had a lot of fun with the fellows from here on. They thought they had seen some mountains until they saw these. Two engines had a hard time pulling us up. We stopped at Camp Hale. That is some camp. I was really surprised. We rode for more than 30 minutes before we got through the camp. A few minutes later we left there, the conductor told us we were more than 10,000 feet high.

Then it began to snow. The fellows almost went nuts. It really snowed heavy. We stopped at Salida and got off for the first time since we left L.A. We exercised a bit and showed off in front of the town's people. I guess it was the first time many of them had seen Marines.  Shortly after that we passed through the Royal Gorge.  We could see the bridge way up there.  It didn't look like it was wide enough for a person to walk across, let alone drive a car across.  We passed through Canon City and saw the State Pen.  This was about 6:30 P.M. Friday night.  We stopped in Pueblo at about 8:50 P.M.  The train workers went over the train.  Some of the fellows had letters they wanted to mail, but had trouble getting anyone to take them.  One woman worker finally took one and slipped it in a pocket and just in time.  A railroad "dick" came around the corner.  USO girls handed us stuff through the windows.  One pretty red-head took a letter and stuck it inside her dress after she had made sure the Captain or the railroad "dick" wasn't looking.  This was the first of two places we had anything given to us.  I was put on guard duty soon after we left Pueblo.

Saturday morning found us in Kansas.  At first it was snow.  Then it was rain, then floods.  I have seen pictures of floods, and I have read about them.  Here and for the following three days I saw the floods in reality.  I didn't like what I saw.  We got to within seven miles of Kansas City and had to back up 20 miles and stay all night.  The tracks were washed out.  Miles upon miles, as far as we could see, there was nothing but water.  There was so much water, even the catfish were climbing the trees and sending out SOS signals.  I saw houses where only the roofs could be seen.  Logs and trees floated with the heavy current with chickens on them.  Animals tried to break down fences to get away from the raging torrents.  Farmers, taking a chance, went out and cut the fences and let the animals go.  I saw a hog swimming with little baby chicks on its back, and a dog carrying a kitten.  Highways and railroads were washed out.  Cars were all along the highways and streets, covered with water.  We could see only the tops of stores and filling stations.  People carried what little they could and tried to get to higher ground.  Children were crying.  Men built sandbag dams and then watched them wash away as soon as they finished.

We ploughed through water mile after mile, just creeping along.  Many times we backed up to take another track.  One freight train passed us and we found it in a heap Sunday morning.  I don't know where the train crew and the two Captains aboard got it, but we had supper Saturday night and breakfast Sunday morning.  It wasn't much, but enough.  The porter on our car swam into a little town, but I don't think he could have brought that much back.  That porter sure took care of us.  He went out of his way to do the little things that mean so much.

One time while we were stopped, we noticed one man

sitting by a window, crying.  Everyone was afraid to go to him and
ask what the trouble was.  After a while, I mustered up enough
nerve and sat down by him.  I asked if there was anything I could
do.  He said no, there wasn't anything anyone could do.  He was
just wondering where his family was.  We all had thought the
reason he was crying was because he was homesick.  He pointed
out the window.  "See those trees?"  I looked and saw what
appeared to be the tops of two huge cottonwoods.  "My house
was in between those two trees.  Where's my wife and kids? What
has become of them?"  I couldn't answer him so I left him to cry
by himself.  I went back to one of the Sgts. and told him. Without
saying a word he got up and went forward.  A few minutes later,
the Sgt. and an officer returned to the car.  The officer took the
man out with him.  I never saw the man again.

We had lunch Sunday in Kansas City.  A big part of the
city was under water.  Sunday night we had no supper.  About
9:30 we pulled into Moberly, Missouri.  The American Legion and
the Service Men's Canteen handed coffee and donuts through the
windows to us.  The rain was coming down in torrents at the time.
Part of their town was under water, too.

We crossed Illinois in the night, and on Monday morning
we were in Indiana.  We passed through Henderson, Ky. about
8:30 A.M.  They had received a heavy rain, but I didn't see any
sign of flooding.

I--in fact of all us--expected to be ordered out to help in
the flood, but we weren't.  I hope I never see anything like that
again. Miles upon miles of water. It was just like riding a train out
into the ocean, except for the people and animals trying to get to
high ground.  The papers here showed a lot of pictures of the
flood and the train wreck.  I suppose the Denver papers did also.
According to the paper I bought, six people were reported dead.
There were many places where we could feel the tracks sink
down.  When we looked down, out the windows, we could see the
water run in on top of the ties.  Things like that made my hair
stand on end.

We saw a lot of interesting things from Kentucky on, in
the way people dressed, the way they talked, the way they
worked.  Hillbillies, colored people, and just plain dirty people.
Some clean.  Most of the buildings, I mean homes, stores,
factories, etc., looked like they would date back to about 1880.
Some of them had never been repaired since they were built, and
paint was unheard of.  Many fields were being plowed with one
mule, with the farmer walking along behind.  We saw no tractors
at all.  We saw one woman milking a cow out in the pasture with a
man on the other side holding the bucket.  One house we went by

had several colored and white adults on the porch.  There must have been 30 or 40 children playing around the yard, all filthy dirty.  The thing that caught our attention, though, was the big hog lying on the porch with little pigs sucking.  That got us all.  This was on Tuesday in Georgia.  All the towns were dirty.  No paved streets.  It was the same way across South Carolina and in North Carolina.  We were asleep when we crossed Tennessee.  Some of us forgot ourselves and made some rather rash remarks about what we were seeing.  We forgot that the Marines are made up of fellows from all over the United States.  We shut up when one of two fellows from that part of the country said it wouldn't always be that way.  I hope he's right.

We arrived at Camp Lejeune at 5 A.M. Wednesday and had roll call and a good breakfast.  After a good hot shower, we hit the sack.

April 29, 1944, Pioneer Company, Engineer Battalion, T.C.

I got my assignment yesterday.  I'm now in the Pioneer Company, under orders from the operations officer.  They have assigned us to construction work.  We are taking the place of the Seabees that moved out of here recently.

At first we were classified as boots, or just out of boot camp.  They were all set to shove us through basic training again.  Then they noticed a large number of the men had seen overseas duty.  So then they called Washington and reclassified the Sgts. and Cpls. as instructors.  After they had reclassified the rest of us, I found myself in the pioneer company which is nothing more than a work crew.

A platoon Sgt. and a Cpl. who were in here a little while ago said they had been in every operations office on the camp trying to find out what we were supposed to be doing here.  According to what they could find out, we, or most of us, will be here about three months.  After that we go to Argentina to build the stadium for the 1945 world Olympics.  I consider it scuttlebutt.

It seems the telephone exchange is too small for long distance calls.  Will try to find out more about it.

May 2, 1944.  I'm feeling just fine except for sunburned back, blisters on my hands, cuts and bruises on my arms and legs.  It seems we are pioneers, all right.  We've spent the last two days cutting trees and brush.  We're cleaning out a fire lane in a jungle a few miles from here.  When I say jungle, I don't mean maybe.  Some of the trees are three feet in diameter.  The undergrowth is so heavy we have to cut our way through.  When we take a step, our feet go down in mud to the ankles.

We're making good use of the checker board and I smoke my pipe with Revelation tobacco which I can get here. I've been offered $30 for my harmonica. I give it a pretty good work out. Sounds like someone has a violin upstairs tonight.

They had a lot of post card pictures at Camp Pendleton of the camp and barracks, but none of them looked like any of the buildings I had anything to do with. I haven't seen any pictures here yet. Of the camp, that is. I've seen lots of <u>others</u>. I'll keep my eyes open and see if I can't get a few of the camp.

According to the papers, the flood waters are getting worse. To think I came through it.

The engineer company I was with went to the tent area. I hope we don't move out there. One of the fellows was telling me today they carry the M1 on guard duty and it's loaded. Here we carry a .45 automatic pistol, loaded.

May 4, 1944. I'm still working, but they took me off of the axe. I spent half a day working on the winch, snaking logs out. For a day and a half now I have worked with concrete mixer.

May 8, 1944. I am now listed as a general carpenter, assigned to refresher school. If I pass the test at the end of the course, I'm supposed to come out a Cpl.

I was assigned Duty NCO yesterday, a job I hoped I would never get. The Duty NCO is on for 24 hours. I think I got about four and a half hours of sleep last night. It's the same as being Sgt. of the Guard. More than one guy has lost his stripe on that job. I made a lot of mistakes, too, but so far I still have my one stripe.

I'm now in the Eng. Co. H & S 29th Marines, just being formed. I don't know much about it. We're standing by to be moved some place. I'm now in the same squad and barrack with a number of NCOs who were instructors at Camp Pendleton. I don't know whether that's good or bad. The 29th Marines are supposed to be trained to make the Raiders look like playboys. I wonder what they want with me in here.

May 11, 1944. I don't know how soon we start to school. So far we are doing some work on a new campsite they say we are supposed to move into. It's just 500 yards from the Atlantic Ocean. I saw the Atlantic for the first time on Wednesday. It looks just like the Pacific. I guess we will live in the jungle in tents. I hope that's wrong.

I thought I would lie down on my bunk and rest a bit last night. It was 7:30 P.M. At 9:55 somebody woke me up and told me to get my clothes off and go to bed right.  I had just raised up and blinked my eyes a few times when I heard a fellow say, "When anybody tells me Negroes and whites go to school together in the North, he is a damned liar."  I jumped out of bed and ran over to the big guy and grabbed him by the shirt front and told him I sat in the same classroom with colored students and I found some colored people were whiter than some whites I knew. They were good students and I wasn't ashamed of having sat in the same classroom with them.

"Now call me a liar," I said.  About that time, I got good awake and realized I was in the South and remembered men had gotten killed for doing less.  The men closed in on us, thinking they were going to see a good fight.

All that happened was the guy says, "Well, I'll be damned."  I turned loose of the guy and went to bed.  And, that's where I'd better go now.  It's late.

May 14, 1944.  I don't know how soon our classes are to start. We may wait until we move to our new campsite.  It's going to be tough living out there.  None of us like it.  Most of the boys have gotten to where they stay on Camp here instead of going out on liberty.  I haven't been out at all.  I have been able to get everything I need here.  They tell me it's too easy to get into trouble.  So many places are restricted to service men.  A guy doesn't know he's in a restricted district until he's picked up by the M.P.s.  I guess it's pretty easy to get into fights, too.  It looks as though the Civil War is still on.

May 15, 1944.  Saw some British officers today.  Also, some Royal Netherlands Marine officers.  I have seen a lot of the Dutch enlisted Marines around here.  They sometimes wear the American Marine uniforms and sometimes their own.  When they wear ours, they have their own insignia on.

May 17, 1944.  I'm getting long just fine.  The weather is beginning to get hot here in the daytime.

Just heard a blast.  Sounded like a boiler or ammunition dump.  They had a dump go up the other day.  I wasn't anywhere near it.  If they had assigned me to demolitions, I think I'd have just given up the ghost.

May 22, 1944.  Here I am, out in the middle of the swamps where I am living in a tent and working hard every day.  Our training has started.  It isn't carpenter school, but combat training.  It's tough, it's rough.  We're going to have night problems too.  If it takes one hour to do it, okay. If it takes all night, we stay until it's finished. I'm wondering what it will be like working our way through this jungle at night. The idea, of course, is to get us ready for the real thing.

Another fellow and I got enough nerve to ask one of the Lts. if we weren't going to get the carpenter schooling. "No," says he, "Since you have been working out here, we have decided we couldn't teach you much along those lines." So, I don't know whether to be mad or glad.

I have to finish this before dark. We have no light in these tents. I bought a flashlight just before we came out, but apparently I'm the only one who has one. So, I'm keeping it under cover so I will have it when I really need it. Of course, I have only the one set of batteries.

I worked on six different jobs yesterday. I was carpenter, plumber, rock hauler, ditch digger, lumberman and water supply man (ran the water purifier). Rode in a jeep for the first time yesterday, too. Now I want to drive one. Maybe I will, too. They took down my name this morning. It seems they need truck drivers. Before we can drive anything, we have to have a Marine Corps driver's license.

Captain Snow is our company commander. He gave us a little pep talk this morning. He said among many other things that he was going to see to it everyman gets to go home before going across. However, we will be allowed only eight days. I have been in only five months. Some of the fellows have been in as much as three years, and haven't gotten a furlough in more than a year.

We are supposed to be going across as the 29th Infantry Regiment. There will be 5400 men altogether. The engineers, of course, are only a part of that. From what I could get of the Captain's talk this morning, we can expect to be pretty well on our way across by the time three months are up.


May 24, 1944. Here I sit with a sore leg. We went out in the devil's playground last night. That's what I call it, anyway. It was 2:00 A.M. when we returned. It was very interesting. We all returned pretty well torn up. My leg is bruised and skinned, but it will be all right in a few days. We now know what men on the islands have been going through. We had to hold on to the fellow in front of us or be lost. I couldn't even see the man I was holding on to. Vines, thorns, trees, stumps, swamps, holes, and anything else you can think of. It was fun, though.

We have some good officers here. Our platoon leader is one of the best.

There are some .50 caliber machine guns going off now somewhere in the brush. In about an hour there's going to be a lot of explosives go off. We're not supposed to be in on that, but I bet we have to duck our heads.

Somebody made a landing on the beach this afternoon. They threw everything they could at those poor guys. They even had airplanes dumping things on them.

May 28, 1944. Here I am after four days. It seems I can't write more often. Seventeen men are going on furlough soon. Apparently I have 15 days coming, but how can I make it there and back and be with you any time? I'd just get there and have to say good-bye as soon as I got through saying hello. Most of the men are waiting until we get back to the west coast to ask for their furloughs. Of course it is possible that we won't go back there, but the Captain said we are to pick up some more of the 29th there.

It's raining hard now. I notice my cot is getting wet. Maybe I should move it, or let down the tent flaps, or something? Before it started raining, it was so hot we could hardly stand it.

Lt. Gray is our platoon leader. He's a tough and rough customer. We all like him. Our platoon Sgt. is the same man I told you about back at Pendleton using me to show the other fellows something about jujitsu. He is only a Pfc. but is up for Sgt. He took us out on the beach yesterday and gave us close order drill, combat conditioning, some instruction in jujitsu, and then we went swimming in the Atlantic. I didn't have any swim trunks, as you know, so I went swimming in my scivy drawers. Under orders, of course. Everything was all right until two officers' wives decided to take a walk and wandered off from the main beach and came down where we were. Three of us were in the same position. We hit the water as soon as we saw them, and Reeling (the platoon Sgt.) went to meet them. I don't know what he told them, but they took a look at us and turned back. The other fellows cussed us for not having trunks. They were nice looking dames.

They had a landing not far from here. Instead of staying in my tent, I went with my squad leader to watch it. At first we couldn't see the eight boats. Then the shore defense sent up flares, and the fireworks started. They threw everything they could get their hands on at those poor guys. It was a lot worse than the infiltration course I went through. We could see the .50 cal. tracers out across the ocean. Irritant smoke, TNT, hand grenades, and a lot of other stuff was thrown at them. Lt. Gray told us later that it was just an idea of what we were going to go through before our training was over if he could arrange it. Hmmm. It seems he wants us to come home again and bring him with us. He's got something there. He wants us to be ready for anything we might run into.

We had another night problem Friday. It proved worthwhile to me. One platoon had a white flag on top of a hill that they were guarding. It was our assignment to slip through the lines of defense and get the flag without being seen. When we were seen, they tagged us and we became their prisoners. My squad leader sent me out as scout. I got caught before I could even get a good start. None of us knew, of course, where the flag was. I saw it after I had been caught. It was not more than ten feet from where I was trying to crawl through the brush.

Sgt. Howell was in charge of the defenders. He has been across and has killed a few Japs on his own. I got a good chance to see him work that night. He reminded me of a cat. He would move around without a bit of noise. I could see him only because I knew he was there. He took more than 40 of us prisoners. I was in his squad before they changed everything up. He told me the other day he missed not having me around to pick on.

Sgt. Moorehead has caught some fish that are very interesting. Last night I was pulled out of bed and told to get my flashlight and come on. When we got down to the river, there he was, fishing in the middle of the night. It had taken him three hours to pull something out of the water and he wanted to see what it was. It was a stingaree, a fish that looks like a pancake, and it is two feet across. It has a little short tail which is the stinger. If it stings man, I'm told, it paralyzes him. He had also pulled out a porpoise, a friend to man, I'm told. A drowning man is helped by this animal; it seems it gets under the man and tries to push him up. A few days ago, something was caught that I thought existed in fiction only: a seahorse. I saw it while it was still alive. It died yesterday. It was very interesting. If I hadn't seen it myself, I would never have believed it.

The barber and the bugler for the engineer company went on liberty without permission. The 1st Sgt. took them out in back of the storage tent and had them dig a hole 4'x6'x6' deep. When they were finished, the good Sgt. looked through his desk and found a burned match stick. He told them to put it in the middle of the hole, length-wise, and cover the hole up again. They did it and right now they're trying to live it down. The bugler is a little guy, the smallest man in the company. The barber isn't much bigger.

June 1, 1944. I don't think we should count too much on the

furlough.  Most of the men are getting five to eight days.  One fellow I heard about who lives somewhere in Colorado got 14 days.  I guess I could get it too, but I would have to spend most of the time going there and back.  I might add that this fellow plans on staying over his leave.  If I have to do that, I guess I won't be seeing you.  I haven't been able to talk to anyone at present.  Only 10% of the men can go at one time anyway.  I don't know whether I can get a change of camp furlough or not. Sure hope I can get a furlough before I go across, though.  If I don't, well, I guess we'll live through it.

You should have seen me Monday night:  mud from head to foot.  It was a night problem.  The azimuth led us across some swamps.  As far as I'm concerned, it was very much going too far.  One man was almost lost.  He lost his head, of course, and that does it every time.  No, it wasn't me, but I did get stuck and had to be pulled out by two of the men.  So did the Lt.  I guess you know there was some cussing going on.  I did some myself.  It felt like the devil had a hold on my feet and was pulling me under.  I still haven't been able to get my rifle good and clean.  They had roll call the next morning and 15 men failed to answer.  Some of them came in about an hour later, almost dead.  We were supposed to have another night problem Tuesday night, but everybody was so near dead it was called off.  I guess we have another one tomorrow night.  We're supposed to see some training films tonight.

It isn't as bad here as it might sound.  In a way, a grim way, it's a lot of fun.  It's like going up into the mountains and living in a tent for a few weeks and hunting and fishing.  Well, anyway, it's nice pretending.

I haven't been able to think much about what I want to do after the war.  As I see it though, the important thing right now is getting home.  I know one thing's for sure:  I don't want to leave Denver.  I don't want to move my family out of our house again either.

June 4, 1944.  This camp isn't so good.  Insects?  I've seen insects I never knew existed.  Those well-known mosquitoes are the size of mules.  Those darn things wind up, go a mile or two up into the sky, and like a dive bomber, they hit.  We have mosquito nets now and sleep pretty good at night.

They keep telling us we're going to move from here next week, but at the same time they keep bringing stuff out here.  I worked Thursday in a warehouse at the base.  Fifteen truck loads of stuff were delivered to us here that day.  The stuff we're getting makes me believe we're going to the Pacific.

I just saw the bulletin board. All men will be checked at once to see that all their private affairs are arranged in proper order. This must be done before leaving the continental U.S. Insurance, allotment, will. Great stuff.

Many of the older men have been taken out of the company. I'm now among the oldest. Fifteen new men were brought in yesterday. They were going to OCS (officer candidate school) and failed to make the grade.

One of the Sgts. asked me this morning where I would like to be right now. I told him, "Up in the Rockies playing with the children's mother."

June 9, 1944. Wednesday night we were marched up on the beach and were issued all the junk that would explode that we could carry. Then we dug in. We had orders to repel an enemy that would be making a landing shortly after dark. We got out dago bombs ready to fire and our siren hand grenades ready to throw. Our rifles were loaded, and we had all the rounds we could carry besides, ready to use. We had just gotten settled good when a flare broke high above us and we could see the boats coming in. I never before saw so many boats all at once. As they drew closer, we could hear the motors throbbing. Our orders were to open fire on the green flare.

Somebody goofed. A skyrocket exploded in the air, and of course, that upset the works. The boats were coming close when the water just off-shore heaved and groaned. A tower of water went 200 feet into the air. The explosion shook the entire beach. The green flare went up and we opened fire. Machine guns threw tracers out across the water, right above the boats. The flares showed us only the sailor piloting the boat into the beach.

I lighted my first bomb just as the first ramp let down and the enemy began to stream ashore. The entire beach became alive then. It heaved and sighed. Dirt and sand covered us as my bomb roared away. I had never fired one before and of course got a burned hand. Not bad, though. I couldn't get any more of my bombs to light. Explosives were going off all around me. There were about 400 of us defending the beach. I picked up my whistle grenades and pulled the lighters on them and threw them at the enemy. Grabbing my rifle, I could see men streaming up the beach, and I opened fire. I got off about six rounds when they ran over the embankment and hand-to-hand combat began. One big fellow ran up in front of me and stopped. He asked, "What do we do now?"

I said, "Get back on the beach," and let him have my rifle

butt in the tummy.  He rolled over and over down the sand dune.
Another fellow heaved up in front of me.  Men were fighting all
around me as I met him and shoved him back into the sand.

He recovered quickly and stated flatly, "You have your
orders and I have mine."  We locked horns.  We were pushing
each other around when the order to cease fire came.

That's the way the engineer and pioneer companies of the
29th Marines let the 750 men in Officers' Training School know
what we were.  They didn't get across the defense line, either.  We
were told later every one of those fellows were boxing or
wrestling champions and many were star football players.  They
cussed us as they marched away.  We, of course, stood and
laughed at them.

Something else we didn't know until it was over.  There
were more than 500 men including two generals watching and
observing our activity.  We saw them when they came from under
cover.  Stories are already drifting in from the outside of the
attack and the defense put up by the engineer company.  We were
the only ones to take part in the hand-to-hand combat.  The
pioneers stood and looked at us with their mouths open.

The officers of our company had made it clear we were
not to use any rough stuff.  At the same time, they let it be known
if we let the attackers get past our defense, we were going to be
very sorry.  We knew what they meant, so we put all we had into
it.  Of course, we got cussed and bawled out--until the brass left,
that is.  Then it was a different story.  They were well pleased with
our activity.

Friday night we made a landing of our own.  It didn't work
out the way we expected because of rough waters.

I worked all day today and was put on guard duty a little
while ago and later taken off by a different person.  I think there
are too many bosses around here.  I'm standing by just in case
the Sgt. who put me on the post returns and starts something.
The man who relieved me is checked out on liberty and he also
had guard duty last night.

Speaking of guard duty, last Monday night I was detailed
to work late with the police Sgt.  The rest of the company went up
to the mess hall where they were shown training films.  The
police Sgt. and I were taking some stuff into the supply tent when
the guard came walking right into us.  There's too much time to
think on guard duty.  You just walk and think.  This was just a
young kid.  He had been married just five months.  He had been
kept in the hospital for more than a month for doing just what we
found him doing: crying like a baby.  I guess I'm not the only one.
But I had my cry out.  It hasn't bothered me since.  He admitted to

us that it was happening to him all the time.  He has to report to sick bay every so often for a mental check-up.  That's the way it goes.  We've had it pretty rough this week, too.  I expected several to break under the strain.

So the big push is on in Europe.

I hope I haven't done the wrong thing by taking a chance on waiting for my furlough.  If I have, then we will just have to take it in stride.  I'm trying to get a delay enroute but they don't seem to like the idea.  They don't want to get to the west coast and get orders to shove right on across and have their men all over the country.  I wouldn't be the only on in that fix.  There are a lot of men trying to do the same thing.

I was over in tent city today, where we are supposed to be moving soon.  It's called tent city, but is made up mostly of huts built of compa board.  It will be better than this hell-hole anyway.

According to one of the Sgts., we are to get our promotions when we get 12 miles out to sea.  It doesn't make sense.

July 2, 1944.  Arrived in camp from my furlough Saturday morning.  Tired, but otherwise all right.  We have a new Top Sgt., many other new men.  Everyone was surprised to learn I had six days in Denver and still got back a day early.

I was assigned to fire watch the first thing on my return.  Mile after mile of forest fire.  I could see it on my way in.  I went to work on my gear even though I had such short time before the truck was ready to leave.  Everything had been changed.  I'm now in the 2nd platoon, 3rd squad, and I'm assigned to another tent with five other fellows.  All new but one.  Sgt. Sasso is my platoon Sgt.  I was trying to get ready to go, including pack and bedding, for we were to stay out there.  Sgt. Sasso came along and said he was glad I was in his platoon and he also told me to stay in camp.  I had been cussing myself for checking in so soon.  I thought then I would have plenty of time, so I went to work on my gear; took everything out of my sea bag so I could straighten it out and put it into order.   Then the order came around: "Inspection in ten minutes."  The fellows asked me what the hell I was going to do.  I felt like taking a big jump into the ocean.  I went to work, though.  When the police Sgt. shouted, "Attention!" at the door of the tent, I saw him glance at me and cross his fingers.  Sgt. Howell, who was with the inspecting officer, gave me a worried look, then looked at me again in surprise.  My greens were hanging up where they belonged, my bunk was made up, my sea bag packed and ready for inspection, my shoes, pack, rifle and bucket were under the bunk where they belonged.  My bag that I carried home couldn't be out so it was in the bottom of my sea bag.

The officer walked in, around the center pole and walked out again. Didn't say a word. Don't ask me how I did it; I don't know.

There were only 23 of us left in camp after the rest of the company had gone on fire watch. So--I caught guard duty. Sgt. Sasso was in charge and he put me on the first watch, which I like best. It rained, of course. I got my feet wet. I'm one rugged person.

On my way back from Denver, I stood up all the way from Chicago, except for about eight hours when I had a chair in the club car, gotten for me by a colored barman. Part of the time i couldn't even get into the car and stood on the platform outside with the Army and Navy. When I got into Wilson, I couldn't get on the bus. I arrived in Wilson about 2:30 Friday afternoon. I got on the bus about 6:00 heading for Jacksonville. The driver had a colored family thrown off at one little town by three big cops, and for almost no reason at all. Of course, in the words of the colored people (and I'm wondering if they weren't right), the driver "reaped what he sowed." We had driven less than ten minutes when the motor stopped. It was raining cats and dogs. We stayed there until another bus picked us up. There was the colored family who had been kicked off of our bus.

I got into the base at midnight. Met a couple of fellows I knew and went with them to their barrack and spent the rest of the night in an empty bunk. Had breakfast on the base, shaved and showered, caught a ride with a Lt. out to the beach, and here I am, expecting Sgt. Sasso to stop me writing any minute and give me some work to do.

They tell me the forest fire started from a tracer bullet. It sure cleaned out the jungle.

A big bulldozer is making a lotta noise breaking into my thoughts. You should see the equipment we have out here now. i can't figure out what they are going to do with all of it. There's a little tiny bulldozer, designed to be carried on an airplane. Just think of a full-grown man riding in the little wagon and you know what it looks like in action. Well, maybe it isn't quite that bad. It's a handy thing.


July 9, 1944. I'm plenty busy. We've moved into tent city. According to what we've been told, we won't be here long. We're loading our equipment and supplies onto the train. It sounds like California will be our next stop, but I'm not sure. All men who are on furloughs have been sent telegrams to get back. We've been working day and night. We're told we have done in three days what the other companies in the 29th took three weeks to do. This is real work. I did mostly carpenter work, building boxes and crates. We worked from 5 A.M. until 11 or 12 P.M., taking time out only for eating.

July 12, 1944. A few of the men who were over the hill (AWOL) [absent without leave] came back. There were about 30 Cpls. They tell me they're no longer Cpls. At the present time, they're cleaning up the head.

We've been ordered to buy enough toilet supplies to last across the country and the ocean. The PX didn't have all we were supposed to get.

At last we're about caught up with the work. About all we have to do now is get some of our personal gear packed. I'm pretty sure we're going to California I don't believe we'll be there long. I think we leave here Saturday. If this is the last letter you get from me for a while, don't let it worry you. I'll be all right.

We've received our overseas shots. We don't have Captain Snow any more. Our new C.O. is from Denver, too. I see him digging the <u>Denver Post</u> out of the GI can after I have thrown it out.

Pfc. Fred T. Klemm on Guadalcanal, 1944 or 1945

July 16, 1944.  Here I am, on the train, crossing the country again. This time we're going the southern route.  We will be going through Texas, almost in my old stomping ground if not right through it.  We're supposed to go through Little Rock, Arkansas, too.  We're now in Alabama.  It's hard to write on the train.  It's getting late, so I won't be able to write much tonight.  We have four hours of classes every day aboard the train.

I think you can expect me to be on my way across the ocean inside a month.  If we stay more than a month in California, it will surprise me.  We're prepared for the trip, although I don't feel I have had as much training as I should have.  They tell us we will receive advanced engineer training over there somewhere before we go into the fighting front.  My new address is:  Eng. Co., 29th Marines (Reinf), FMF, Linda Vista, Camp Elliott, San Diego, Calif.

July 18, 1944.  I recall many things from my childhood as we pass through Lubbock and Littlefield, Texas.  I don't know why we switched off our course to come so far north, but I'm glad we did. We were in Fort Worth early this morning when I went on guard duty.  Then we went down to Brownwood, almost in the middle of Texas.  Now we're going northwest from Littlefield by the setting sun.  The fellows have been asking a lot of questions, most of which I can't answer.  Some of the green crops I don't know. Some I know I should know, but can't think of the names.  Cotton I know.  In Georgia and Alabama it was full of blossoms, but here it hasn't quite reached that stage.  It's sure green though.

This country has filled in.  I can still look for miles upon miles, but now there are a lot of houses.  I remember the highway running along the tracks from Lubbock to Littlefield.  I haven't seen any prairie-dog towns yet.  There are a lot more trees than there used to be.  Mesquite bushes are the same.  Cotton gins are the same.  I remember seeing the Farmers' Co-operative Gin in Littlefield.  There didn't used to be so many tractors.

This morning while we were stopped in Brownwood, a little boy walked along the tracks, looking us over good.  When he got to me, he stopped and looked at me hard.  Everybody in the car had his head out a window to see what he could see.  I asked the boy what town we were in.  He didn't answer me, but stood looking at me.  The fellows looked at me and I looked at them, but nobody said anything.  I looked back at the boy to see if there was something wrong with him.  Then he asked, "Are you a Jap?"  I don't think the fellows will ever get through teasing me. We found out later the porter had told him we were Japs.

July 21, 1944. We arrived here yesterday afternoon, safe and sound. We're in a tent camp about a mile from Camp Elliott. The weather is a bit chilly. We're pretty high up. Anyway, I haven't seen any swamps.

We were given the word last night we won't be here very long. Our equipment is already being loaded aboard ship. I hear somebody trying to sound a bugle. I don't know how long we will be allowed to write letters, or mail them, I should say. The whole 29th is moving in here.

July 23, 1944. Here it is Sunday. Not much doing today. Most of the fellows have gone on liberty. I was surprised they were allowed to go. Two more groups came in this morning. It won't be long before all 5,400 men will be here. Our C.O. told us that this is the last regiment to form in the U.S. Any men going out now will go in pools as replacements. I wonder what that means?

We worked all day yesterday down at the base, unloading the train. We had chow there too. I haven't eaten such good chow since I left boot camp. The whole place looks the same except it didn't seem to me there were as many men as there were when I came through.

Apparently we are to stand by until they see fit to move us out. I don't think we will get a whole lot of training here. We had a little bit of extended order day before yesterday.

Oh, yes, we were changed up again in our platoons. It changes every so often. This time we were divided up into fire teams. I'm a fire team leader (four men). That calls for a Cpl., or is supposed to. I don't know whether or not they even intend to give us those ratings like they said at first. I haven't heard any more about it.

I hope you aren't worrying about me going across. I'm sure we won't be going into combat for some time after we get across. We need more training and the whole regiment has to learn how to work together. I don't think we'll do it here, although we might.

This whole camp is very poor. They have very little here. The chow halls are terrible. Of course they don't expect to be here very long and won't do any more than they have to toward fixing it up.

We're having a lotta fun from some colored fellows here. They came over to our area the other night and put on some close-order drill for us. We laughed until we hurt. They put some boogy-woogy and a lot of other such stuff into it. They really know their stuff, though. It went on for a couple of hours. Then their officers drove up in a jeep and watched for about a half hour, then had them fall in and march back to their own area. I haven't laughed so much since I have been in the Marine Corps. It was a good show.

From what I can hear, it won't be much longer until the Germans will be out of the fight. Then it won't be long before the Japs will be out of it. That will be the great day.

I see the bugle with the bugler hanging onto it wandering up and down the street. I don't know why, but it might take a notion to go up to that bugler's lips and make a sudden noise. Oh, well.

July 24, 1944. Received package with peanuts, candy, flints, matches, wet stone and razor blades.

I've been unable to talk to any of the officers about the medical care of the family. I'm going to try to arrange for you to get some more money on the allotment, about $10. I won't need it where I'm going.

I worked down at the base again today. The boots were having a parade when we went to chow. I could sure feel for them.

July 26, 1944. I'm tired but otherwise OK. We worked all day yesterday and last night. We hit the sack about 8 A.M. I've gotten about four hours sleep so far. They keep calling us out for this and that. The time is short. We've turned in our greens and made out overseas address cards. The cards will be sent as soon as they receive word we have arrived safe.

July 29, 1944. We're changing camps. It'll be some time before you hear from me again. I have to go out on a working party tonight. We had a parade review today. I didn't know there were so many men in this camp. I haven't been able to get anything on the medical care. I waited too long to get some money changed to allotment.

July 30, 1944. I was glad to be able to use the telephone. It was sure nice to hear my wife's voice.

Aug. 12, 1944. Pfc. Fred T. Klemm, Eng. Co., 29th Marines (Reinf) FMF FPO San Francisco, Calif. I'm all right. I got seasick the second day out, but it didn't last long. I'm all right now, but just the same, I would give almost anything to see some land. When I get back home, I'm going to the top of Pike's Peak just to see how far I can get from the ocean.  I'm a shellback now. [Someone who has crossed the equator by ship.]  We're having a good time.

Can't tell anyone where I am, where I'm going, nor what I'm doing.  I'm told I'm now Cpl.  It will be a regimental warrant and is subject to confirmation in six months.

Aug. 19, 1944.  I'm getting along fine in my new home.

Aug. 21, 1944.  I'm sending a paper home to be filed away for me. It will give a general idea where I am.  I haven't been able to find out anything about the medical care.  Everyone is pretty busy. It's too bad there isn't a Navy hospital in Denver.  If there was, we wouldn't have to worry about it.  It's hot here, but otherwise it isn't bad.

Aug. 23, 1944.  I'm getting along OK.  My platoon Sgt. had told me I had made Cpl. but apparently it was a mistake.  I think I know where I fell down and I'm going to try and make it up.  The officers had me up for an interview the other night.  I don't think they thought much of my work before I came into the Marines.  I don't know whether they are going to rate me on the T.O. [Table of Organization] as a carpenter or not.  I hope so; I like carpentry.

I've seen lots of black natives.  One of them had red hair. I've eaten coconuts; there are lots of them here.  The Japs were here, but are gone now.  The only time it's cool here is when it rains.

Sept. 1, 1944.  Here I am on an island in the South Pacific and the same as ever.  It's been raining here and it cooled off a bit.  I'm still working as a carpenter.  I'm working with a man who really knows carpenter work.  I've learned quite a lot from him.

Sept. 12, 1944.  Well, we have the day off.  Feels pretty good. Hey, we had fresh fried eggs for supper last night.  We're doing all right.

The guys here in the tent are horsing around and are making me forget what I wanted to write.  They mixed up a lot of junk and made a candle.  I don't know what all they have in it.  I was expecting it to explode, but it appears to be burning all right.

The only thing I can say about where I'm at is that I'm in the South Pacific.  The censors are my own company officers. Nice fellows, too.  But they don't let anything go out that isn't supposed to.  After all, that's their job.

I think I'll go for a swim.  These guys are driving me nuts.

They're shoving some riddles at me now.

Sept. 16, 1944. I'm getting along just fine. I'm still listed as a carpenter. The last few days I've been driving a truck. It has proven rather exciting. These trucks are a lot different from anything I ever drove before. It's a pretty good sized truck I've been hauling gravel with (2½ tons). It has ten wheels and double reduction gears. Five forward gears, front wheel drive. I had a little trouble getting the Marine Corps driver's permit, but I have it now. I can do carpenter work now in the daytime and drive at night if need be. Hope it isn't needed too often, though.

Sept. 22, 1944. Still driving a truck. The men in the tent tease me quite a lot about my driving. It's all a lot of bunk, of course. They've been telling me what to write. If I put it in, I'll land in the brig and how.

Sept. 23, 1944. I received a <u>Collier's</u> today. It's good to get something to look at from the good old states. I'm getting along just fine. Can't complain at all. Am enclosing a money order for $25.

Sept. 23, 1944. There are lots of coconut trees here as well as bananas. The natives are friendly but black as charcoal. The biggest things to worry about are the little green mosquitoes. I don't like those things at all. I go on guard duty at 11 P.M.

Oct. 23, 1944. I'm getting along just fine except for being homesick.

Last night I went to the show. It was good and I enjoyed myself. When I returned to my tent, I spent a good half-hour getting my bunk fixed up again. My pad had been rolled up, my sea bag was on top of the rolled-up pad. My rifle was on top of that. My shoes had been put on the cot with several pairs of pliers, bayonets, rifle rods, and, to tip it off, all the beer bottles they could find in the area. Great shipmates I have. I took some of the beer bottles and put them on one man's stomach and put his arms around them. He didn't wake up. When the bugle blew this morning, there was a loud crash and it's a good thing there weren't any women around.

The natives here are not like those shown in the movies. One wouldn't even try to compare them with the Hollywood idea of a South Seas native. They're black as midnight, and they wear nothing above the waist. Men and women wear close-cut hair. Some have blond or red hair, but most have black. All like to smoke: pipes, cigars, cigarettes. Even the little kids smoke. I talked to one native several times. According to him, everything we do is wrong.

The 2nd platoon, of which I'm a member, has just returned from a problem that took several days. We worked very hard. We really had a good time. We ate C and K rations but we fared rather well. The only thing that bothered me were the mosquitoes, lizards, ants, bugs and other insects that worked their way into my sack. The lizards played around the pup tent we lived in. I drove a truck and had it easier than any of the other fellows.

I received 20% more pay for overseas duty. There should be $10 more in the allotment. There's very little to spend money on here.


Nov. 4, 1944. We just came out on top with an inspection. It was the fastest inspection I've ever had. I'm still trying to catch my breath.

I wanted to go to the show tonight, but it's raining. I guess I'll have to make it another time.

The heat here sticks my envelopes shut. I have to spend much time getting them unstuck.

I'm not getting schooling on carpenter work. It's infantry, mostly. I've been getting quite a lot of engineering.

It's been ten months now and I've been overseas three months.


Nov. 10, 1944. We've been getting some training in demolition. We went out into the field today and set off a lot of stuff that made a lotta noise. I made it better than I thought I would. I just can't help but shake when I'm working with it though.

So President Roosevelt won again. He won't run again. We'll see if I'm right.

The natives wear just a plain piece of cloth wrapped around the waist. They like colored print. There's nothing else that they wear.


Nov. 15, 1944. The soil here is quite rich. Almost anything you would grow in your garden will grow here. There's a lot of stuff growing in the jungle: some vegetation and some insects. I've seen some of the strangest things I have ever seen. I don't know the names for all of them. But for an example: when I was sleeping out on the ground a couple of weeks ago, I had a bug, I guess it could be called a bug, crawl into my sack with me. I was up out of there in no time flat. When I turned my flashlight on it, it looked like a green leaf off of a shrub or tree. It was about two inches long and slimy. It was green on top and white on the bottom, and it had two very small legs on each end. I couldn't find a head. After I looked at it, it crawled away.

There's lots of fruit besides coconuts. Most of it grows wild, and some is poisonous and some is eatable. I don't know the difference so I don't eat any.

Nov. 16, 1944. I drove the water truck today. Filled all the water tanks for showers and sprinkled the street to keep the dust down. No very exciting.

We just had a Jewish fellow that sleeps in the tent here explain some things to us about the Jews and the things they do. It was rather interesting. He doesn't believe there are any Jews left alive in Poland. He had some grandparents over there.

Pfc. Fred T. Klemm, Co. C 6th Eng. Bn. <u>6</u>th Mar. Div.

Nov. 19, 1944. I received a V-mail letter this evening. It was easy to read which is more than I can say for one I saw that was received by one of the other fellows. He couldn't even tell who it was from.

I just got back from the movie. One nice thing, we don't have to pay to see the movies. We built a stage and screen in between two hills. We use gas cans to sit on. It's really a nice outdoor theater. They had a party to celebrate. Everyone had a good time, including me who didn't go. A certain number of men have to stay in camp.

I had my six bottles of beer and drove a truck all day. Don't worry, I didn't drink it all at once. In fact, I still had two to finish off tonight. The party was yesterday. We had liberty today. I spent part of the time pinning up pictures onto a piece of pressboard. My favorite pin-up pictures: pictures of my family.

I'm no longer a carpenter on the TO. I'm now listed as a truck driver. Anyway, I won't be driving the wrong nail. Not much chance of making Cpl. I'm not worried about that; all I want to do is get the war over and get home.

Nov. 24, 1944. Thanksgiving Day we did no work. We had a most wonderful meal. It was really good: turkey, dressing, cranberry sauce, mince pie, cake, mashed potatoes, gravy, hard candy, assorted nuts, and a lot of stuff I can't remember. I drove a truck all day and this evening we had a drill contest between the companies. We came in last. We had a lecture on booby traps tonight. Those things are a good test for a man's wits.

Nov. 26, 1944. I received the watch along with many goodies. I went down to the Seabee area to see a show tonight. It was the first time I had been there. They had a fire eater on the stage, but the wind was blowing enough that he burned his face.

Nov. 28, 1944. I'm getting along just fine, except tonight I have a headache. I fired the .50 cal. machine gun today. They make a terrific noise. We fired from the beach out over the water, using barrels as targets. I sank one of them. This evening we had school on booby traps. Last Sunday we fired hand grenades and rifle grenades. We fired the rifle grenades from our M1s just like firing a regular round. I thought it would jar my eye-teeth out.

It's swell to be wearing a watch again. I sure missed it.

Dec. 3, 1944. It's beginning to rain and I have clothes on the line. That's the way it goes. Well, it's raining too hard to go get them now. They tell me it's about time for the rainy season to start.

I'm trying to get my truck painted while it's being worked on. I haven't been able to drive my own truck for some time. They have a hard time getting parts. We have only camouflage paint so it's a job.

Dec. 7, 1944. Tomorrow is my birthday. Almost didn't remember. I'm getting along just the same. Still trying to paint my truck. I have it almost finished.

Dec. 9, 1944. I failed to put an address or return on my last letter and the censor sent for me. I couldn't figure what I was being sent for. Silly thing to do.

I spent my birthday trying to paint the under-part of my truck. Very trying indeed. The under-part of a truck doesn't look very charming.

Dec. 12, 1944. We're going on a training problem. I expect to be kept rather busy.

Dec. 19, 1944. We got back off our problem all right. From what I could see of it, everything went off all right. I drove a truck and had it much easier than most. I slept in the truck. When I got back to my cot, I had to hang my legs over the end before I could go to sleep.

Our water purification men did a wonderful job. The bridgers did all right and the road builders with their bulldozers did a good job. Of course the truck drivers did all right, too. Try hiding a big truck sometime so that it can't be seen from any side or from the air. It was my biggest job. It's a lotta fun. You can back the darn thing into the jungle, but there's still the hole where it went in. Then when you pull out, if you hear a clanking noise, it will be vines around the drive shaft. On backing in, if you should stop suddenly, you have hit a tree or stump. Find yourself another place. And don't pick a place where some infantryman has crawled into it and dug himself a foxhole. Of course, if you get stuck in the mud, there's always one of the bulldozers standing by to pull you out. So you see, you have no worry in the world. The rest of the time, you just sit in your truck until it's wanted. Driving a truck isn't so bad. I have no complaint. We go out on another problem the 24th.

We got some shots in the arms tonight. That makes ten I've gotten since I've been in the Corps. I have guard duty at 2 A.M. so I'd best get some rest.

Much of the edibles I received in packages can't be eaten. Cake and fudge are always ruined.

Dec. 24, 1944. All's quiet and peaceful. It's Christmas Eve. We have until Tuesday off. We didn't go out into the field like I thought we would. We're supposed to go sometime in January. The sun is shining bright. It doesn't seem right not to see snow on Christmas.

Dec. 25, 1944. South Pacific. Christmas Day. We had turkey with all the trimmings. One of the fellows received a radio through the mail. Right now the tent is full of fellows, and there is some western music on the radio.

One of the fellows just remarked it has been five months since we left the states. In two more days it will have been one year since I left Denver. It seems like ten. I think the five months I've been overseas have aged me a year.

Dec. 28, 1944. I've been trying to get a picture of the 6th Div. shoulder patch, but haven't had any success. If I'm not mistaken, it has a blue background. The sword is white, the 6 is gold, the ring around it is red, and the wording is gold.

Dec. 31, 1944. A cat (I don't know where it came from) just chased something under a board under my sack. I raised the board up so the cat could get at whatever it was, but it took off across the tent with the cat right behind it. It looked like a mouse, but it was moving so fast I couldn't tell for sure. The cat has come back. It is gray with black stripes, a tiger cat perhaps. It didn't catch whatever it was under the board.

A land crab just came in one side of the tent, looked me over, and moved out the other side. The cat didn't bother it.

I had no chow at lunch time and supper at 7 P.M. I got in pretty late because I helped take some equipment out for our problem. I saw a big tractor slide off a trailer and turn over. It went completely over and stopped on the other side. The man on top was lucky to jump clear. After it had been righted, it started right up and pulled itself out of the ditch. It was bent up a bit, of course. It weighs something like 20 tons. (It was an International TD 18.) Just another one of those things that happen.

Jan. 7, 1945. I have my own truck out of the garage now. It started to rain a little this Sunday morning, but apparently changed its mind. The sun is shining and it's rather hot.

There's some opera music coming over the radio right now. We get lots of good programs. There's Bob Hope, Charlie McCarthy, Amos & Andy, Fiber McGee & Molly and many others. They come over an Army station here on the island.

Jan. 15, 1945. I'm too darn far from home right now, a lot farther than I ever expected to be. As a kid, I used to dream of traveling over the world and see how people lived in other countries. I still haven't seen very much, but right now I yearn for the over-stuffed chair in the living room with my book and pipe and having my family near me.

Jan. 17, 1945. I just finished putting a top on my truck. It's about time. None came with it. These trucks do not have cabs on them. They have tops that fold up if desired. I finally got hold of an old frame and some canvas and went to work. By the time I finished, I had three fellows helping me. If they hadn't helped, I would still be working on into next week. At least it keeps out the hot sun and the rain.

My watch is keeping perfect time, but I broke the band.

Jan. 22, 1945. I'm listening to a radio program that has two Hollywood stars up to answer questions. It's rather interesting. I've had a very bad cold. It's been hard to get rid of. It seems funny to be getting a cold down here.

I'm still driving a truck. I need to do a little more work on it, then it'll be ready. I get a lotta jokes shoved my direction about me and my truck. Almost everybody calls me "Seven Miles an Hour Klemm." I got that when my truck's brakes were bad and I refused to drive too fast. I figure I have the duration and six months in here anyway, so why get in a hurry? The one time I want to get in a hurry is when I head back to the States and home.

Feb. 3, 1945.  We were out in the field last night.  It rained of course and, as usual, men crawled under my truck.  Can't blame them.  Had one in the cab with me.  The truck wouldn't cover all of them, so a lot of men got wet.  Oh, well, all a part of the job. I'm just lucky to have the truck to be in.  It would be a dirty trick to start the motor while those guys are under the truck.  Yes, it would be too dirty.

Feb. 10, 1945.  Yes, there are white women on this island.  The Red Cross, USO, Army and Navy nurses.  I haven't even said hello to any of them.  There are a few down at the Service Center the enlisted men can tell their troubles to.  There is always a big crowd around them and anyway, I don't have any troubles to tell them. There are WACs here too [Women's Army Corps].  Our new company commander and his wife are here.  She is a member of the Red Cross.  We see women go down the road every now and then.  The Service Center is pretty well supplied.  It's several miles from here, so we are given permission to drive as many trucks as are needed to take everyone who wants to go.  There's a big club where the women are.  The radio station is down there.  There are four different movies that I know of, and a big PX, plus service buildings such as the Red Cross, Chaplain, library, etc.  They also have basketball courts, boxing rings, and other things.  It's quite a place.  I haven't noticed any radios or phonographs down there, but then we have the combination in our own mess hall.  We sometimes pick up very dim stations in the States late at night. It's a big cabinet model with an automatic record changer.

Feb. 15, 1945.  A couple of fellows came in last night with harmonicas.  We didn't quit until the lights went out.

Feb. 20, 1945.  My wedding anniversary--seven years.
	I worked all night the last two nights, but got to sack in during the days, so it wasn't so bad.
	Enclosing money order for $30.

March 8, 1945.  The additional $10 a month was never changed from my pay to the allotment.  As long as I can send money orders, it doesn't make a lot of difference.
	I walked out the other day and saw to my pleasant surprise a complete, beautiful rainbow in all its glory across the end of the island.  The time was--9:15 P.M.

April 1, 1945.  Easter Sunday and April Fool's Day.  First waves hit the beach on Okinawa.  [Invasion.]  I'm now in combat on Okinawa right in Japan's back door and so far I haven't received a scratch.  I'm driving a truck and they keep me pretty busy.

The natives here are pro-Jap.  Some are friendly and some are not.  The island itself is very beautiful with pine trees and lots of gardens.  The natives are very industrious, especially the women.  They carry babies on their backs and go to work. I've seen them carry loads on their heads I doubt I could push in a wheelbarrow.

The roads are very narrow and we with our big trucks and other big equipment have a pretty hard time of it.  Natives either walk or ride horses.  In the larger towns, the natives are quite modern and wear western dress.  Some wear the kimono, and some of those are very beautiful.

I was on Guadalcanal before coming here.  This island is much more beautiful.

Just heard President Roosevelt died.


April 21, 1945.  Okinawa.  I'm sharing a pup tent with a Cpl.  Our tent is right in front of a tomb housing the bones of many Jap ancestors.  There are many of these tombs on the island.  The bones of these ancestors are put into earthen urns and sealed in these tombs.  Some of the urns are very beautiful.

We're unable to leave our pup tents at night.  If we did, we would stand a very good chance of being shot.  I've been up in the front lines a number of times.  Several times I've been ahead of the front lines.  A few times, I've been scared silly.  As yet I've not fired my rifle.

Every time I go any place, I'm driving a truck.  It went into the garage today.  Yes, it's in the garage often.  But it's a good truck and it has a good driver.  With narrow roads, dust, land mines, blown-up bridges and road blocks, my truck and I take a beating.

I'm sending some invasion money and one Jap bill.  It's 50 sen, worth one nickel in American money.  We had to turn all our American money in for the invasion money.  Ten sen is worth one penny, one yen is worth one dime.  I am also including some postage stamps and some ration stamps.  I have some coins I don't know the value of, and a couple of medals I will send at another time.

The air raid siren blew a few minutes ago.  Right now, I

hear some machine gun and rifle fire.  The Cpl. and I are looking at each other and wondering if we hadn't better put out our light. We made sure it couldn't be seen from outside, but just the same, we don't like the sound of things.

There are a lot of things here I would like to send home, but I'm not going out of the way to gather them up.  I figure the best souvenir I can take back home with me is me.  There are too many booby traps and snipers.

April 29, 1945.  The big fight with the Japs is over in our area. We still can't get out at night, though.  There are still a few strays out.

I have grown a mustache; now isn't that interesting?

May 5, 1945.  I had a little hard luck the other day.  I was pulling a bulldozer on a flatbed trailer behind my truck on muddy roads right after a hard rain.  I went around a curve and felt the truck and trailer slip.  When I got my brakes set and went back to take a look, the earth had given way.  The bulldozer was upside down in the China Sea at the bottom of a 20-foot embankment.  Nobody was hurt, but if the dozer had been chained on, the trailer, track and all would have gone over.  It was a brand new piece of equipment that had just been issued to the company. It had never been worked.  It was pulled out that same night and they almost have it in working order again.  The engine started up as soon as they got it back onto its tracks.  I sure hated that it happened, but I can't see how I could have avoided it.  I thought I was going to face a court martial, but the only thing that happened was a "cussing out" by the stripe-happy Cpl.

We've been hearing about Ernie Pyle [journalist].  He was killed on an island not far from here.

Over here the women do all the work while the men sit around and talk.  Oh, they drink saki, too.  I took two gulps of the stuff and was sick for two days.  I'm not drinking any more.

May 5, 1945.  It's pretty quiet right now.  We've changed camp sights and have moved farther south.  We're helping the Army a bit.  I'm enclosing a song one of our fellows wrote.  It expresses our feelings pretty close.  The fight has been tougher in the south than in the north part of the island.  I can't get much news here. You know more about what we're really doing than we do ourselves.  If you could put a bit of the news in your letters, we would all like it. You know, a few things they say about what the Marines are doing.

Okinawa, May 5, 1945

Sung to the tune of "Rum and Coca Cola"

We're all done up Nago Way
Now we go to Naha Bay,
Chasing nambus with grenades
Doggies laugh at Marine Corps way.
(chorus)

(2)
Got down there the first of May
Took Naha the second day
Doggies they all felt so sad
While Marines, they fight like mad.
(chorus)

(3)
Marines fight fast and never slow
Then real soon the Japs they go
While the Doggies make big show
Dancing at the U.S.O.
(chorus)

(4)
Marines come back all full of mud
Itching with the Chinese crud
Doggies, they're all cleaned up nice
While Marines are picking lice.
(chorus)

(5)
When the island's all secure
Army heads for U.S. shore
Marines move on and take some more
That's what ends the U.S. war.

Chorus
Drinking saki on Okinawa
Saki on Okinawa
Saki on Okinawa
Fighting for the Army soldier.


saki = Japanese whisky
nambu = machine gun
Naha = largest city here
Naga = second largest city
Doggie = nickname for soldier

May 16, 1945. Okinawa. I'm getting along as well as can be expected. I'm now on the southern part of the island but two miles behind the lines. I'm camped with the heavy equipment crew on the edge of Machinato Airstrip (censored and inserted later). I'm the only truck driver with them. Sometimes they keep me pretty busy. They call me "Lucky Teeter," after the famous stunt driver. So far I've been able to get there and back, but I can get into some of the durnest messes any truck driver ever got into.

Our own artillery is making me jump as it fires. Pretty often we receive some over here from the Japs. I've been up to the edge of Naha (censored). It is pretty hot around there and I don't go up any more than I have to. My sack is in a fairly safe place. I've a concrete wall on two sides and a dirt and rock pile on the third. One end is open. It is just big enough for me to sleep in. The top is covered over with boards and old canvas. I can just sit up in it. I have a straw mat to put my blankets on.

We're all glad that Germany has surrendered. All we hope now is it'll soon be over out this way. Where we are, it's rough. No one is receiving packages and I haven't received my pay for more than two months. I don't expect any right soon. I don't need any money, though. The only thing I have to pay for is stamps. The Red Cross gives us shaving gear, tobacco, cigarettes, candy, chewing gum, writing paper, etc.

May 24, 1945. Okinawa. I'm still with the heavy equipment. We moved from the airstrip back with the company. It got too hot for us there. The night before we left a shell landed within ten feet of where I was trying to sleep. The only thing that saved me was a concrete wall about three feet high. I hugged the base of that wall like I never hugged anything before--well, anyway, I got pretty close to it when I heard the shell coming. It threw dirt and rocks all over me. I could hear the shrapnel whine through the air. I've seen men get hit by those. They are something to hide from. The only safe place is under the ground.

I'm back now where it's half-way safe. The only thing that has happened to me so far is that when I stuck my head into a tool box on the truck, I let the steel lid fall on my head. A corpsman nearby fixed me up and everything is all right.

I'm sleeping in a hammock now. Every time I get into it, I expect it to turn over with me, but so far it hasn't. The hammock has a top on it and netting on the sides. I shut myself in with a zipper. I have a tarp thrown over the whole thing and when it rains like it has been the last two days, the water runs right through under me.  Me, I'm as dry as I would ever want to be.  Pity the boys trying to sleep in foxholes.

It's really muddy this morning although the sun is shining. I drove approximately 12 miles this morning in two and one-half hours and used ten gallons of gas.

I haven't heard anything about two planes making suicide dives at any of our bridges.

Our boys do take quite a beating.  Just the other night some of them ran into some trouble and it was raining, too.  They were trying to work on a bridge in the dark.

The 1st and 6th Marine Divisions are on Okinawa.  I haven't heard anything about any others having landed here. There are several Army divisions here.  The 27th traded positions with us when we moved south.  They are now in the north end of the island.

We're glad to receive clippings from home.  The people at home know more about what we're doing than we do.  We don't think the news sources give us enough credit or say enough about what we're doing.  The infantry, of course, is doing a tough job. And what a job.

June 3, 1945.  Okinawa.  I was wondering yesterday as I read a letter from my mother telling me to "Remember the Lord's Day" just when Sunday was supposed to be.  Today I find that yesterday was Sunday and today is Monday.  I think Tuesday is supposed to follow.  It's hard to keep up with the days of the week and the day of the month.  And the month, too, as far as that is concerned.  Oh well, whatever the day is, it's raining again. My truck is broken down.  I'm living in a school building in the edge of Naha and am all right.  Living in the school house built of reinforced concrete isn't so bad.  It's a lot better than living in a muddy foxhole like so many of the boys are doing.

The fellows still call me Lucky Teeter.  The other day, I ran off into a well on the side of the road.  I also got stuck in a mud puddle on the side of a hill just back of the front lines and a big bulldozer broke two big chains pulling me out.  Yes, I guess I have been pretty lucky.  But then I have three most wonderful ladies riding in the seat with me.  I can't see them but I know they're there.

I've had lots of flats lately.  You know I have never used strong language, but I put it to use several times while I was trying to repair the heavy things in the rain and mud.  If I let the tire fall flat on the ground, three men couldn't pick it up again. We had to get a bar and pry it up.  That's _mud_.  Try to jack up the truck and the jack sinks out of sight.  Then I take a shovel and dig it out again.  The stuff sticks to the shovel and can't be thrown off.  Oh well, such is war.  It's still raining and I see a truck out there up to its axles in mud.

A big mountain of beef just came in here and I told him he would have to get out because he had bats in the belfry.  He conked me on the skull and told me to behave.  I guess I will, too, because he's twice my size.

June 12, 1945.  Okinawa.  I received some packages.  The pocket knife will come in handy.  It's something I've been needing.

I'm still all right and going strong.  So far I have been working every day since we hit the island.  I was informed a little while ago I had to take at least one day a week off.

June 19, 1945.  Okinawa.  We're now camped near Naha Airfield. We're living in tents, but it isn't a bad camp site.  I'm getting along just fine.

June 30, 1945.  Okinawa.  We're not working so hard right now and I have a little time to myself.  It sounds like I might get into heavy equipment pretty soon.  I've been trying to ever since I left boot camp.  I've been getting a little practice on a bulldozer and maybe I'll make the grade.

Chapter 6: Guam

July 18, 1945.  Somewhere in the Pacific.  We're now on another island.  We haven't been told yet we can tell the name.  It's a fairly nice camp.  Needs a lotta work done on it, but we have wooden decks in the tents, electric lights and showers.

I made heavy equipment.  Will start learning how to operate some of the equipment soon now.  My next pay will be $138.67.

July 22, 1945.  I've been assigned to operate the motor patrol (a one-man grader).  I think I'm going to like it all right.  There are lots of handles to pull and a lot of places for my eyes to be all at once, but I'll make it.  The motor patrol is used for finish work and maintenance mostly.  It has a diesel engine.

July 25, 1945.  We're having to do some work on the motor patrol in the shop.  I know what you're going to say.  My truck was in the garage quite often and now the motor patrol.  Well, just don't you worry about it.  It was already in bad shape.

Am enclosing money order for $100.

July 29, 1945.  The news sounded good for getting home, then it went sour.

I'm beginning to learn how to handle the motor patrol.  My instructor knows what he's doing and tells me all he can.

I don't expect to get home until the war with the Japs is over.

A little native boy came into the tent the other day while I was playing my harmonica.  He asked me to let him play.  So I let him have the harp.  He blew on it a couple of times.  The fellows in the tent put their hands over their ears and I didn't know what to expect.  He turned it over and read out loud:  "Marine Band."  Then he played the Marine hymn all the way through.  Of course I wasn't the only one surprised.  Men came over from the other tents.  The boy played a number of American folk and western tunes.  He told us that a Marine had taught him to play the instrument in about a week's time.  He snowed me so far under I won't be able to get out for a long time.  He is about ten years old.

We get beer and coke now and there are shows in several different movie areas.  We can take our pick and go every night if we want to.  The chow is getting better, too.

Aug. 2, 1945.  Colorado Day is Aug. 5th here.  I'm going to see if I can't get down to where all the fun will be.  I understand they're preparing quite a program for the Colorado men.

Aug. 3, 1945.  I went to see a show last night starring Betty Grable.  There wasn't any story to it at all, but what legs.  There's another good one on tonight that I think I'll take in.  One of the fellows is walking back and forth in front of the tent waiting for me.

Aug. 8, 1945.  I had a good time on Colorado Day.  I didn't find anyone I knew.  There were a lot of men from Denver, but all strangers to me.  I understand the whole thing is being printed in the <u>Denver Post</u>.  There was a native woman who gave a talk about Colorado.  Four young native girls sang Colorado songs.  It was really good.  Of course Colorado Day is Aug. 1st, but it was held on Aug. 5th so more fellows could attend.  I believe I saw every branch of the military service represented.

Aug. 9, 1945.  I heard some more good news today.  Sounds like things are going pretty good.  According to the radio, where I get most of my news, Russia has entered the war with the Japs.

I heard about the plane hitting the Empire State building last Sunday.  I saw some pictures of it tonight.

Everything is still the same with me.  I'm still working with the grader.  I like to tease the big brute who's instructing me.  He's twice as big as I am and when he lets go with that rumbling voice of his, it can be heard for blocks.  He knows his stuff though.

Aug. 13, 1945.  The news is looking up.  I've been so excited the last two days I stuck pretty close to the radios in the area. Even though the fight may end soon, it does not mean I will be home soon.  I expect to have several months out here yet. Anyway, it is nice to know the fight is over and I have a much better chance of getting home.

They took our motor patrol yesterday and gave it to another company.  I understand we are to get a new one.  In the mean time, I'm working around the dozers and other heavy equipment.

Aug. 18, 1945.  Well, I did finally land in the shop myself.  I'm now in the 6th Division hospital.  Nothing to worry about, though.  I didn't move fast enough and let a bulldozer roll onto my right leg. There are no bones broken, just a bruised leg.  I'm receiving wonderful treatment and will be out of here in a few days.

Everything is under control.

I don't know when I'll be home. I expect it to be some months yet.

Lava soap comes in handy. They don't sell it in the PX.

Aug. 23, 1945. I got out of the hospital yesterday afternoon. My leg is still a bit sore and I limp around like an old man. But it is healing right up. I was in the hospital six days. I received fine treatment.

Upon my return to duty, I found I had been put back to doing carpenter work. I guess I was just meant to be a carpenter. I don't mind, though. I like working with wood. Taking me out of the heavy equipment had nothing to do with the accident. Half of the men were taken out. I'd been expecting to be put driving nails again because we had a reclassification test not long ago, and that was the way it sounded to me. It won't hurt me to do a little carpenter work again.

Aug. 27, 1945. I'm pretty tired tonight. I had four hours of guard duty last night, went to school this morning, and another four hours of guard duty this afternoon. There's no work at all to guard duty, but for some reason I feel worse than if I had worked hard the entire time.

The entire guard had to go in this evening and recite the general orders to the officer of the day. I made it. I couldn't look him in the eye while I did it, though. If I had, I would have forgotten every line. Why is it a guy gets in that condition?

My leg is still a little sore, but it is healing all right.

Sept. 2, 1945. V-J Day! Wonderful. It's all over. I'm sure glad. I heard the broadcast of the signing of the surrender papers. Shortly afterward, we were issued beer and coke, all for free. We have all day tomorrow off. All I want now is to get home.

Sept. 5, 1945. Everything is under control. I've been trying to get ready for the general's inspection. When the general inspects, everything has to be just so.

I started working nights with last night being the first. Don't worry, it is really nice. It isn't so hot and I have the days off. I only work five and a half hours each night.

The accident happened on Aug. 16th. I had just received my pay and had gone out to do some work in the compound with the motor grader. The motor patrol has to be pulled to get it started because the starter won't work. A Lt. was operating the dozer with which he was going to pull me. I got the chain fastened, but the first attempt broke the chain. He backed up and stopped. I went in between the two pieces of equipment to refasten the chain. Just as I bent over, I heard the dozer move. I looked back and saw it coming for me. I jumped, but wasn't fast enough. I caught my right leg between the tract of the dozer and the front wheel of the grader. How the dozer got in motion is something I don't know. I'm sure it wasn't on purpose. The Lt. rushed me to sick bay and the doctor there rushed me to the 6th Mar. Div. hospital where it was found the leg was not broken, only bruised. You know what happens when you push in on the side of a rubber ball--that side will stay in. That's the way the muscle in the back of my leg was. It's healing up, though. I couldn't kneel on it the other day when we were firing our rifles. I fired the kneeling position in the sitting position.

There were no nurses in the hospital. Navy corpsmen take their place. I shaved off my mustache while in the hospital, and when I returned to my area, no one knew me. The MPs at the gate called the top Sgt. to identify me before they would let me in.

The reason there was a doctor at sick bay was because he was giving shots to the men. My company was marched up while I was inside. When I was carried out on a stretcher, the fellows thought I had passed out because of the shot. They didn't know about the accident until I returned from the hospital.

We're building shipping crates at night.


Sept. 6, 1945. Censorship is off. I can now record a number of things I wouldn't before. I'm on Guam. Where I'm going from here is something I don't know. I'm thinking of China, however. I don't know when I'll be going home. The point system means little to the Marine Corps. It's mostly for the Army. Some with 85 points have left. I have 61 points. I expect the system to change.

I've been so mad at times I didn't give a damn what happened. It was and still is the way we are being treated by the officers. I can see now why the Marines are so good: they are so mad when they go into battle, they don't care whether they live or die. Too many died on Okinawa.

I didn't make Cpl. when I expected to because I refused to kiss a bunch of butts. I kept out of the brig by the skin of my teeth. I was all for banging some skulls of some dirty rats. The NCOs have improved quite a lot since the operation, but the officers are beginning to throw their dirt around again. I have become quite a yardbird. I do just what I am told to do, nothing more. That's the way it's going to be until I get out. I bang ears just enough to keep on the desirable detail, and that's all.

There's a lotta things about the operation on Okinawa I'll

never be able to tell anyone. But I've seen, heard and done things I never dreamed of ever doing. It might surprise to you learn my stomach turned upside down just once, and that was when I saw my first dead Jap. You have never smelled anything bad until you have smelled war. It's hell.

As a truck driver, I was able to get around a lot more than I would have otherwise. I also got out of a lot of undesirable details. I saw and got into more than I really should have. More than once I have driven along roads that were covered by Jap weapons. Little spurts of dust jumping up in front of me and mortor shells exploding on either side of me was nothing unusual.

The time they first started calling me Lucky Teeter was shortly after I had driven through an ammunition and fuel dump that was on fire and exploding. I went through unharmed, although I had three flats. I changed them the following morning.

I could get into some of the durnest jams. One time I ran off into a well. Another time I got stuck in the mud with a generals' jeep right behind me. Mortors were falling all around us. The MPs were all over me. Of course it was all my fault. You know me, I leaned back in my seat and puffed on my pipe. One of the generals got out of the jeep and came up and talked to me-- where was I from, etc. All quite in order. I sat and waited while the MPs sweated and the Seabee dozer was coming to pull us out.

When the dozer pulled up to hitch on to my truck, the MPs got all excited. They were to get the generals' jeep out first. A Seabee officer told them to go to hell and hitched on to me. The MPs hitched the jeep on to the back of my truck and we were pulled out together. The truck tires made ruts wider than the jeep. The general doing the driving couldn't hold it in one rut, and the vehicle bounced back and forth from one rut to the other and finally threw one general out into the mud. This, of course, was unknown to me and the dozer operator. The general thrown out wasn't hurt, just covered with mud. When we first learned what was happening was when the general ran up along side of the truck yelling. I almost busted a gut in a effort to keep from laughing right out loud. Gen. Shepard, who was driving the jeep, looked at me and said, "Well, laugh, damn it, laugh." Then I didn't want to anymore. Gen. Shepard was commander of the 6th Mar. Div. The other general with him was General Clements, vice commander.

Another time the MPs had us all stopped because of a mud hole the Seabees were working on. After I had sat in the same place for four and a half hours, trucks and jeeps were lined up two miles behind me. I took off down the railroad track when the MPs had walked back a piece. The whole two miles of vehicles followed. I got through and got away before the MPs caught on. I heard later the MPs were trying to find out who I was. Those who knew wouldn't tell. As far as they were concerned, Lucky Teeter had done it again. That's the way they started the tale when they got into camp: Lucky Teeter has done it again.

One officer, I don't remember his name, told me when I got on the road to hell, he wanted to be aboard. I'd be sure to run into something to keep me from getting there.

Sept. 7, 1945. We passed the general's inspection with flying colors so got the rest of the day off. We were issued six cans of beer. I drank two cans and woke up four hours later, just in time for evening chow. I wasn't drunk but I got sleepy. I wasn't the only one.

Gen. MacArthur, as the story goes, said no Marines would be used to regain the Philippines, but the 11th Marine Regiment was on Leyte. You read so much in the papers and hear on the radio about what the Army is doing in the Pacific. According to rumor, the Army has done very little. When you hear something about what the Yanks or Americans have done in the Pacific, you can bet your boots the Marines had a big hand in it, but they make it sound as though the Army did it all. On Okinawa, according to the story I got, the 27th Army Division was driven out into the ocean. The 1st Marine Division went to their rescue. The 27th was sent to the north end where we, the 6th Marine Division, had just finished up. We took their place in the south end. The 6th Mar. Div. secured more than two-thirds of the island by themselves. The 27th Army Div., according to rumor, couldn't even hold Nago after we had secured it. The Japs slipped through and ran them out. Gen. Geiger, a Marine, was in command, replacing Gen. Buckner who had been relieved of his command before he was killed. He told the 27th to win Nago back or die. They got it back just before we left the island.

Generally, the Marines have a great respect for the 96th Army Division and the 96th fought side by side right down the center of the island during the entire operation.

The toughest and most important points on the island were taken by the Marines: Nago, Shuri, Naha, Naha Airfield, Orako Peninsula, Itoman and many others. On the radio reports we heard, it was reported the Yanks had taken the points.

The 2nd Bn. 4th Marine Regiment, 6th Marine Division was the first to enter Japan. They were in there several days before any of MacArthur's men entered Tokyo Bay. The Army men found their colors [flag] they had lost at the outbreak of the war in a museum in Tokyo.  Maybe I'm just bitter.  Anyway, we don't rate very well.  We get, it appears, the dirty assignments every time.

To get back to some of the happenings on Okinawa.  We built what we believe is the longest Bailey bridge built by the Marines in the Pacific, right in the middle of Naha.  The Japs were on one side and the Marines on the other.  C Co. of the 6th Engineers was in between.  We worked day and night under mortor and artillery fire.  The bridge is 380' long and was fired on several times while we were working on it.  We constructed it in two days.

I saw men get killed on the Machinato airstrip.  We slept there several nights, or tried to.  Some of the Japs tried to make landings there at night.  I could see everything that could be seen.  The Japs were caught between two destroyers.  The flood lights would pick out the little landing boats and the machine guns would open up.  Not even one Jap got ashore.  In one way, we were glad and yet again we were disappointed.  We were ready and waiting for them.

There was no part of the operation that went off the way I had expected to see it.  I saw men playing baseball with shells exploding in the outfield.  We watched a movie one night while an air raid went on overhead.  We could either look at the movie or watch the air fight.  I saw two of the suicide planes dive into a ship.  I also saw many of the planes shot down.  While the hot part of the action was on, the film was turned off.  When it subsided, the movie was turned on again and the show would go on.

Bailey Bridge, Okinawa, built by the 6th Engineers

The infantry had the hardest job of all. They had to stay in the front lines day and night. The engineers could work in the front lines in the daytime generally and withdraw at night.

I don't want to ever hear anybody say anything against the Navy Corpsmen that were with the Marines. They did a most wonderful job.

The civilians I saw come out of the hills from the Jap lines were thousands and thousands of walking zombies.

Sept. 8, 1945. I've been taken off night work and am working days now. My watch is doing fine. I made a band that should last for awhile out of some metal from a Jap plane. The bomber had been shot down on Naha Airfield. I'm wearing a Jap belt for work and I have a Jap raincoat.

Sept. 13, 1945. It's raining and there's just enough breeze blowing to make the dampness go through the body.

Nobody here as yet knows where we are going. It still seems like China though. China is one country that has always fascinated me and as long as I have to be in here a few months yet I think I wouldn't mind seeing it.

They still don't know what the engineers are or how to use them. They never had engineers in the Marine Corps before this war broke out.

Sept. 14, 1945. Our work has let up quite a bit. We go over and sit on the bench and wait for orders. The ships are being loaded. We're going some place. I hope I get to go on an LST [Landing Ship, Transport]. I like them better than APAs [Attack Transport]. I was on an APA on the way from Guadalcanal to Okinawa. A large number of us had no bunks. We slept any place we could find space enough to park the body for the night. Usually, we could find a place on an upper deck. And, of course, it had to rain. I stole a cot two nights and slept under a landing boat. That was all right until somebody stole the cot from me. So I slept on a coil of rope (line, in sailor talk) or on some crates, or just the steel deck in a corner where nobody would step on me. Of course when they had general quarters everybody had to be below. Down there you were lucky if you found enough space to lean up against the bulkhead.

General quarters is when they have an air raid alert or submarine alert. Men assigned to guns go to them on the double and everybody else goes below. There was at least one every night, and sometimes several. I saw my first plane shot down the night before we got to Okinawa. I was on deck when I wasn't supposed to be, but I wanted to see what was going on. It's a good chance to get killed, of course. The real scene is from the shore. It's really something to see the ships fight off the invading planes.

There are three lugs in here who are very drunk. They had $7 among them three of them. They spent it all. They still have $7 and are now arguing about where they got it.


Sept. 15, 1945. Guam. There isn't as much noise in here as there was last night.

We were given the word today that our letters are being spot censored. There are certain things they don't want us to write about: troop movements, etc. But they won't be telling us where we are going until we at least get aboard ship and maybe not until we get there.

The officers are the source of a big part of our scuttlebutt. Some real humdingers can come out, too. I'm hearing more than my share right now. We five guys here in the tent got to wondering just what did happen to scuttlebutt. So we made up a harmless story. The following morning, each of us told the story just once. The following evening it came back to us right here in the tent. The nut that told it to us had gotten it from a friend in the battalion office. It couldn't be anything but the straight dope. So there you are. I don't believe anything until it happens, and I can't even be sure then.


Sept. 17, 1945. Guam. When I tried to get in O.C.S. I was told no because I was too old and I was married.


Sept. 19, 1945. I'm now on dock guard, a twenty-four-hour watch. We will go back to camp at noon when we are relieved. There are five of us, a Cpl. and four guards.

The mail clerk sent our mail down to us. "Torpedo" Johnson wants to know how "our" wife is getting along. He's the Cpl. of the guard here with us.

If some kind of bonus is paid when I get out, it will help pay for a car.


Sept. 20, 1945. Guam. According to the scuttlebutt, I won't have enough money where we're going anyway, so it won't make much difference how much I take along. I'll be darned if I'm going to pay $20 for a package of cigarettes. (It turned out to be Chinese dollars and some of the fellows paid more than $100 for a package of cigarettes.)

I was able to get hold of some official pictures of the Okinawa operation. I've seen the type of action that took place in all of these pictures, and I took part in many of them. When the picture was taken of the collapsed bridge, my truck and I were trapped on the wrong side. The bridge had been weakened by Jap demolition charges, but it hadn't broken down when I got there. It was a concrete, reinforced with steel. I was stopped by an MP on duty with orders not to allow any trucks across. Only jeeps and recons had permission to cross. Only a few minutes before, I had driven through a school yard with exploding ammo and fuel. The smoke from the burning fuel could be seen by us from the bridge. So, seeing as how I was an engineer, driving an engineer truck loaded with vital supplies, this MP decided I should know what I was doing. He asked me to go down under the bridge and take a look to see if I thought it would hold the weight of the truck. I went and looked. I didn't know whether it would or wouldn't, but I told him it looked good to me.

The MP ordered the men on the truck to get off and walk across. They refused. I gave the order and they climbed down. They grumbled as they walked across and waited on the other side. I put the truck in low gear, left the door on my side open so I could jump if necessary and moved slowly across the bridge. On the other side, the fellows climbed back on board.

A jeep driven by an engineer officer stopped near the MP. I knew the officer and he knew me. He was in charge of putting the Bailey bridge shown in the picture across the weakened concrete span. He saw the truck on the other side from him and I got a good cursing and so did the MP. Then the officer decides he wants to cross with the jeep. Three men got in with him. There were a number of men on the bridge assembling the Bailey. When the jeep reached about half-way, the bridge gave way. We went back and took a look at the sickening sight in the canyon below. The engineer officer in charge wouldn't let the corpsmen take care of him until all the other injured had been cared for. One man had a slab of concrete lying edgewise across his middle. There was no way to care for him. He begged for someone to shoot him. The officer in charge saw me looking down from above and ordered me to get going with the water supply equipment. He said the men at the submarine base were out of pure water to drink.

We got back on the truck and headed in the direction of the submarine base at the north end of the island. On our way, we caught up with a bulldozer halted at a channel in the road that had been dug out by the Japs to halt traffic. We found several more after that. This dozer operator wasn't to be stopped. Smaller than most men, he was attempting to bridge the channel with anything he could find available: boards, old telephone poles, etc., all which were scrawny and weak. We helped him place the debris across the channel to form treads for the track of the TD 18 bulldozer.  He then lined the tractor up with the two paths, threw in the clutch and jumped off the back.  Standing in back of the equipment, he watched it cross to the other side.  As soon as it had cleared, he ran across, jumped onto the back end, threw the tractor in high, and took off down the road.

The men with me helped straighten the boards and poles so they would line up with the wheels on the truck and I drove across without incident.  We had a trailer hitched on behind, too.

I couldn't use lights to drive by when night came.  There was no room and we didn't know the password for that day.  As we came to the other channels in the road, we found the dozer operator had paved the way.  Two of the men sat on the front fenders, watching for the channels, as we could easily drive off into one in the darkness.

We finally reached where the amphibians were firing at the Japs in the hills.  By singing the Marine Hymn and other American songs as loud as we could, we made it safely into the camp.  We were halted by one of the men we were looking for.  I slept in the bed of the truck that night, covered with an old canvas.  The following morning nine of my ten tires were flat.

I saw the submarine base only from a distance.  Drank some coffee from a tin can heated on an oil fire and repaired my flats.  Around 10 A.M. I headed back.  When I reached the collapsed concrete bridge, I found my work was cut out for me.  Many trucks were bringing supplies as far as the bridge.  Men then carried them on their backs down into the canyon and up the other side where they stacked them to be loaded onto my truck.  Since my truck was the only one, I drove day and night until the Bailey was completed.  Why didn't my shotgun driver relieve me? I never had one during the entire operation.

It's hell driving at night over strange roads without lights. One truck, no guards, just one scared driver with orders to get the supplies through.


Sept. 23, 1945.  They took down some of the tents to take along with us.  Of course, I had to be living in one and am now in another tent with the bugler.  He's just a young punk.  I can put my arm out and he can just almost walk under it.  We even had to turn in our cots and pads.  I now have two blankets on the deck in the tent.

I understand the men with 70 points are leaving tomorrow. They're going to a transit center where they will wait for passage. We are standing by for word to move out for China. It's different this time. There isn't that fear of what the future will bring at the end of the trip.  I feel no dread of the trip at all.  The men are all cheerful.

We expect it to be cooler there, so are pretty well prepared.  For the first time in a large number of years I have some longies.  They are the drawers type and a sweatshirt is worn for the top.  It's going to have to get a lot cooler than I think it will for me to wear them.  We also have flannel and a field jacket.

Sept. 27, 1945.  Guam.  Here I am in the middle of the harbor at Guam.  I don't know why they brought us aboard so soon.  We aren't expected to put out to sea until Oct. 2nd.  I don't like living aboard these ships because it's too crowded.  There are about 12,000 Marines aboard besides the sailors.  We're on an APA.  The chow is good but the dining room is too small.

Okinawa (USMC postcard)

Demolished bridge, Okinawa (USMC postcard)

Raising the flag on Okinawa (from the book Okinawa by Nichols)

72

Oct. 8, 1945.  Enroute.  We left Guam a week ago yesterday, Sunday.  We went to Saipan, where we laid over two days and now we are pretty close to where we are going.  The officers don't tell us much, but they say Chih-Fou, China.  The only thing we can find close to that on the map we have is spelled Chefoo. We think it's the same place, but we aren't sure.  The location is right across from Korea.  We think the reason the officers don't tell us is that they don't know either.

The points have been lowered to 60 and I have 63.  It looks like <u>I might</u> get home for Christmas.

The trip so far hasn't been too bad.  The ship is crowded. I walk from one end of the ship to the other to find a place to sit down and read and then when I get settled they have some kind of a drill.  It is getting cooler day by day.  The one thing that bothers me most is that somebody keeps rocking the ship.  So far I haven't gotten seasick.  But if that dirty rat that is shoving the bow of the boat up and down and sometimes sideways doesn't quit pretty soon I'm going to get mad.

There are some birds flying around, so we must be close to land although we can't see any.  We're supposed to get there tomorrow or the next day.

I don't know just what my job is going to be.  I understand we're to build an airstrip, work over some three hundred miles of road, and furnish water.  That will be the job of the engineers. The infantry has another job.

The men are all in good spirits.  It isn't at all like it was before.  I have read something like 40 books since I've been aboard.  I've been able to keep off all the details but one: cleaning up the compartment where we sleep.  It takes about an hour and a half.  We have a great deal of spare time aboard ship. Some sleep, some play cards, most read, some write letters. Some get around in little groups and talk and tell dirty stories, etc.  Of course there is always at least one who stands and just stares out over the water.

Yesterday we had a couple of hours entertainment.  We have the 29th band aboard and also some guitar players and singers.  It was a pretty nice Sunday afternoon concert.  Oh yes, movies every night in the mess hall:  one night for troops and the next night for ship's company.


Oct. 14, 1945.  Tsingtao, China.  I'm enjoying myself for the first time since I've been in the Pacific.  This is really something.  You can read about it in books and papers and hear it on the radio, but you have to really see it to get the full grasp. I don't mean seeing it in the movies.

The orders were changed and we came ashore here for the first time yesterday. I was put on guard duty the first thing and am still on guard. It isn't bad. The officers are too busy having a good time themselves to pay much attention to us. I'm on guard in what will apparently be our equipment compound near the docks. The real camp area is in a school some distance uptown. One of the drivers dropped by and took a Cpl. and me for a ride. He was headed for the camp area but got lost and drove all over. I'm glad he got lost. There is supposed to be a million and a quarter people in this one town, and I believe it. The part we saw was dirty and smelled as bad as the stockyards. There is a geisha house on the corner of every block and three or four in between. We were invited inside several times right from the street. The Chinese had a big celebration last night. We could hear them way down where we were on guard. Of course we wanted to see what was going on, and that's why we took the ride at first chance, hoping no one would care. Nobody even knew about it. The Navy is the only one to have legal liberty. Liquor is every place. Kids would walk and stick the bottles in the jeep in our faces. The people do not stick to the sidewalks, but are all over the streets, which are rather rough. Sanitation is very poor. In fact, I have yet to see any.

Most of the buildings are brick or concrete. I'm at present writing this in a concrete building that at one time was an office. The door just blew shut and I, taken by surprise, dived for a window, only to find it had steel bars over it. I hadn't noticed that before. There apparently is no danger here, but---. Oh well. The streets are decorated like downtown Denver at Christmas. U.S., China, English, and Russian flags are every place.

Many of the people wear the western dress. Most wear the Chinese costumes. I don't know just what they're called. We're not supposed to buy anything, and aren't supposed to drink or eat anything native.

They didn't even issue us any food. We (the guard) stole some "C" rations last night and a little while ago a truck driver dropped by with some "10 in 1" rations he got from a quartermaster by telling a white lie. They're the best. They have to be cooked, but we can take care of that. We also got a truckload of lumber from the docks. We keep a fire going all night. My feet felt like they were going to freeze off last night. We're living in a tent we put up.

Chinese soldiers directing traffic in the streets stop all

traffic so we can pass. There are people every place. They have a Nationalist soldier on one intersection and on the next there is a Communist. It makes a lotta sense. The people clapped their hands and shouted as we passed. A great many stuck their thumbs in the air and shouted some words. I haven't yet found out what it means, but we have been assured it's all right. I stuck my thumb up in the air right back at them, and the whole crowd laughed and laughed. Apparently they liked it. I'm trying to beat the sundown and am writing too fast. I got two letters yesterday when we first came ashore and one of the water supply men brought me another one a little while ago.

I hadn't heard the 10th Army had been disbanded. We're still a part of the III Amph. Corp. I have heard no more official word on the 60-point men going home. The officers seem to think replacements will have to be brought in first. By that time, the whole unit will be in the States. I don't know what we're doing here in the first place. So far everybody is running around like a chicken with its head off. Everybody seems to be in a daze. The only job for the engineers is water supply.

The whole thing is rather exciting. Don't worry about me and the geisha girls. That's out. The drinking is out except for one thing: if I get a chance, I want to taste the Russian vodka, just to see what it tastes like. They have warned us it is the only safe drink here.

I just happened to think of the town where we were supposed to go, Chih-Fou. I don't know why the orders were changed, but there we were supposed to build an airfield.

Oct. 17, 1945. Tsingtao, China. I'm still on guard in the equipment compound. We're getting hot chow now. The pioneer company set up a mess hall in what used to be some kind of an office. The rest of our company came off the ship yesterday. I think they plan on keeping us down here which is all right by me. They're throwing too much dirt at the boys in the school: bed checks, close order drill and such.

I found out sticking your thumb in the air means "good" and sticking you little finger in the air means "no good." We have some of the coolies working for us here. They clean up the camp area, saw wood, clean our mess gear, etc. We give them some chow and they're happy. Seems like they would rather work than eat.

We've seen some of the trains leave and come in. If there is a square inch on that train, it has a man or woman on it. They hang on the sides, on the roofs, all over the engine, even the stack.

I don't know when I'll get orders to come home. Our names have been turned in and we're due to board ship as soon as we get the order. It may be days, weeks, or months. I'm hoping to be home by Christmas.

A Staff Sgt. was just here and read off a number of papers to us on what we can and can't do, what kind of clothes we're to wear, what we can buy, and what we can pay for it, where we can go on liberty, what we can take pictures of and what we can't. None of the geisha houses were restricted. How do you like that? The NCO is to line us up before we go on liberty and see to it we are dressed correctly and have our pass, etc. I'll be glad when I can again go, dress, talk and do as I please.

Oct. 20, 1945. Tsingtao, China. How would you like to pay $1500 for one meal? That's what I paid for a steak dinner the night before last. That's approximately 75¢ in American money. Am enclosing $100 bill. That was my first liberty, and Cpl. Milke and I thought we would like to just walk around and see what we could see. Had this dinner in a Russian cafe. It was really something to see white women dressed in American dress. Only the blonde could speak English, and of course the men were packed around her ten deep.

We walked around for about four hours. Street vendors tried to sell us everything they could pick up. Most of it was worthless but cost plenty. Small boys and girls were out trying to get us into the whore houses. Each had a dirty picture to show so we would understand what they were talking about. The price was one dollar. The next time I go out, if I do, I'll take a ricksha ride just to see what it is like. There are hundreds of them clamoring for you to ride.

We're standing by now for a parade on the 25th. Nobody will go home before that. After that, anything can happen. It's to be quite a large parade. Some Jap general is to surrender to Gen. Shepard.

I'm receiving letters now I should have gotten while aboard ship.

We're still in the equipment yard. I was up at the school where the rest of the company is staying. I'll stay down here just as long as I'm in China. Nuts to that stuff. They're all crowded into one big room.

I visited the heating plant, an Ideal cast iron sectional boiler. That was all; no return pump. The return water is allowed to run outside. When the water in the boiler gets low, more water is added with a hand pump. No temperature controls; just a valve on each radiator. Boiler is hand-fired with coal. Half a dozen coolies were working hard but accomplishing nothing.  The #1 man walked around with his hands behind his back, and a big smile on his face.  I walked in, nodded to him, and started looking around.  I guess he thought I was somebody.  He started shouting at the coolies and they moved around a little faster.  I didn't stay long.

It's a nice brick building, covering almost a square block, with semi-indirect lighting throughout and window ventilation.  It was used for a Jap boy's school, for ages 8 to 15.  There was a large playground in back.

Oct. 26, 1945.  I'm still here, waiting and hoping.  I thought maybe we would be sent aboard ship after the parade and the surrendering of the Jap troops here in this part of China.  So far the only thing I've heard is that points have been lowered to 50.

They tell me the parade and surrender went off all right.  I wasn't there.  Glad I wasn't, too.  They had quite a long way to march and then they were so far back they couldn't see what was going on.  A Cpl. and two Pfcs were left in the compound and I happened to be one of them.  Some of the boys think I banged ears to get out of going, but I didn't have anything to do with it.

I haven't gone on liberty any more.  I just can't see there is anything to go for.  They're beginning to close down some of the geisha houses.  That is, they are off limits to Marines.  The doctors made a check and didn't like what they found.

Today some of the boys got $3600 in Chinese money for one American.  I can't see how that can keep up.  It seems more than one agency is printing the stuff.  Sooner or later something has to pop.

It got cold enough for me to put on the longies they issued.  They're all right, too.  Nice and warm.

I go on guard at 2 A.M., so should get some sleep. Tomorrow night I'll be on from 6 to 8 P.M.  We just keep rotating. It's now a quarter till 9 P.M.  My watch is working fine.  At first I was the only one here with a watch, so it went the rounds with all the guards.  Now some of the boys have bought watches from the Chinese.

It's hard to explain about these people.  The other day at noon I had some food left over.  Of course, as usual, I proceeded to dump it in the G.I. can.  As soon as I got through the door from the mess hall, I was attacked.  Hands from all directions grabbed for the food in the mess gear.  They cleaned it out.  The same thing happened to the men behind me.  Ragged and dirty, boys and old men stood waiting with hungry eyes for the next man to see if he had anything left.  We're not supposed to give food to them outright, although we sometimes do. I notice some of the Marines quit eating before they are finished. When I was on liberty the one time, I saw small children with apparently no home fixing mats on the sidewalks to sleep on.

Oct. 29, 1945. Two Chinese soldiers were in here with one of their war dogs. They stopped in for a visit. I started to pet the dog--- Grrr. I made a hasty retreat. One of the men could speak a little English. We invited them into the tent and I guess they saw a lot of things they had never seen before. They sure could ask a lot of questions. Of course, we had a lot for them, too.

We have one little black and white dog that came to live with us soon after we landed. We call him Poochie. He's a nice little dog. He's about six inches high. Yesterday some of the truck drivers brought in two little puppies they found some place without a mother. One of them is pure black with white fee, so we call him Blackout. The other is black and white with brown spots on the head, and we call him Whitey. Poochie likes to play with the little ones, but he's too rough with them and they set up a big whine. Of course we can't stand that and slap Poochie which makes him whine.

The other night I started playing my harmonica and before I knew it, Poochie was up in my lap trying to take the harmonica away from me. We have a hard time getting food for the dogs, but they are a lot of fun.

There are a large number of coolies outside the tent here unloading barbed wire and are causing quite a lot of trouble. I have to go on duty in another hour. The sentry now on duty is having trouble keeping the coolies out of our equipment.

Oct. 31, 1945. I'm glad to hear so many of the boys are returning to their homes. I'm glad somebody is getting to get out. I haven't heard any more about going home. Cpl. Ford, who had 69 points, boarded ship yesterday. The rest of us went up to the school tonight and drew clothes: green coat, fur-lines vest, etc.

Shepard House, a club for enlisted men, is to be dedicated tomorrow afternoon by the general himself. The American Red Cross has invited all enlisted men.

Nov. 4, 1945. I went on liberty last night with Cpl. Milke and had supper at a Chinese place. When I say it was good, I don't mean maybe. It was so good we made a second complete order: two orders of steak, french fries, eggs, cake and ice cream. The whole thing for the two of us was $5,800. They were giving $3100 in exchange for one American last night, which means the meal cost us about a dollar a piece.

We had our pictures taken before we went to chow and Milke left his watch to be repaired. After we ate, we went and got our pictures. Shortly after, I bought a little cap for each of the girls. They have a lot of color in them. They're supposed to be silk, but I say they are rayon.

After that we went to get rickshas to take us back to the compound. They wanted an American dollar a piece. We finally got three to say they would take us for $400 Chinese dollars. Milke got settled in his all right, but me, of course it would have to be me, I had a problem. We couldn't use three rickshas. I had one coolie on each arm pulling me toward his ricksha. Milke sat back and laughed. He was all ready to go. I finally had to throw one of them away from me. As for the ricksha ride, it was all right. I know one thing for sure: that little man, who didn't come up to the five feet mark, really earned his $400 Chinese dollars. It was a good two miles and he ran most of the way.

Mr. Yong was here watching me write. Right now he's playing cards with one of the men. Mr. Yong is a young Chinese, some kind of guard for the railroad here. He's been washing our clothes, etc. He came in here the other day while the boys were playing cards and made motions he wanted to play. He can't speak or understand English, but is learning fast. The boys decided they would get him in a poker game and take the money away from him that we could see sticking out all over him. I don't know how many thousand he had, but they wanted to clean him out. I didn't think it was fair and let them know it. I didn't need to have been afraid for him. Right now the boys are yelling for pay day. He cleaned out every one of them.

I haven't heard any more about going home. I think, however, from what is happening, I don't need to expect to be home for Christmas. I think next spring would be more likely. The Civil War here in China isn't helping things any. I can't see why we should help China out with her problems. I can't see why it should be our worry. But then here we are.


Nov. 6, 1945. We were finally relieved of our guard duty at the compound. The Colonel made an inspection and walked through our tents. Even though we had tried to make it as pleasant looking as possible, he decided it wasn't a very nice place for men to be living and ordered Lt. Poppe, our present company C.O., to move us out. So I'm now in the school house with the rest of the company. They built double-decker bunks and of course I have a top one. I don't think it will be bad, though. I don't like all the G.I. stuff, but it can't be helped. I was satisfied down there: no inspections, drill, or dirty details.

Very few of us have received any mail for the last six or eight days. We're wondering what's happened to it.

Nov. 9, 1945. Tsingtao, China. Still no mail. We are all wondering and some are worried. I haven't seen anything to get worried about yet. I'm just getting impatient, tired, and disgusted.

Nobody seems to know why we're here, what we're supposed to do or when we're supposed to leave. They run around finding stuff to be done just to keep the men busy. As for me, I'm getting my share of guard duty.

I'm getting very impatient. I can't see the reason for all this fooling around: close order drill, including fancy drills, fancy rifle manual and drills. I can't put my heart into something like that at all. Of course, it ends up with the Lt. pulling me out to go through it alone. I'm not the only one though. Surprising, too, it's the older men having trouble. I'm one of the older ones. I don't believe there are more than ten or 12 men more than 28 years old in this company. Right now I feel like I'm forty.

Nov. 10, 1945. Today is the Marine Corps birthday. There are ceremonies downtown, and we each got a can of beer at chow time to celebrate. It's the first state-side beer we have had since we left Guam.

Guard duty is much the same here as anywhere, except in combat of course. This is informal guard we have here. There's the Officer of the Day. He can be a Warrant Officer, 2nd Lt., 1st Lt., or Captain. He's in charge of the entire camp area as well as the guard, for 24 hours. He or the commanding officer gives all orders concerning the guard. Then there's the commander of the guard, but we don't always have one. We do have a Sgt. of the guard, the NCO in charge of the entire guard. He sees to it that all orders of the commanding officer, the officer of the day, and any other officers that are concerned with the guard are carried out. Then there are three Cpls. of the guard, and each Cpl. is in charge of a relief. In this case there are three reliefs. It's up to each Cpl. to place a guard on each post to see to it that each guard carries out his orders. There are two types of orders: the General Orders which every man has to know by memory and the special orders which are written and posted on each post. A sentry does not have to know these word for word, but he must be able to tell the Officer of the Day or anyone else concerned what they are, on command. There are 11 General Orders. That's what I had all the trouble with in boot camp.

Here the most important special order is to keep the

Chinese out and the Marines in. The hardest is to keep the Marines in.

In addition to the guards mentioned, there is the supernumerary. One or more men stand by in case one man on post has trouble and needs help or gets sick. That happened the other night. An extra man was put on gate 5 when the sentry on duty was shot at. The guard is on duty for 24 hours, and we cannot leave the area during that time. I've seen times when the entire guard was called out and stayed on post during the entire night. Anything can happen.

At guard mount or muster, every guard or man concerned with the guard is present. The Officer of the Day inspects every man. In this case, we wear green trousers, wool or khaki shirt, helmet liner, leggings and field shoes, plus a rifle and cartridge belt with two canteens, bayonet, and first aid packet. All articles must be clean, and the man must have a clean shave, clean finger nails, etc. Oh, don't forget the hair cut. The inspecting officer may inspect the rifle and then ask me to recite one of the General Orders, or he may ask for my rifle number, or how I like the Marine Corps, or if I'm married, or if I have children, or what state I'm from, or he may not ask any questions at all. I have seen an inspecting officer stand in front of one man and make him sweat for ten minutes, asking all kinds of questions. Then he will turn around and bawl him out because he has not buttoned the flap down on the right-hand shirt pocket. During that time, the rest of us are standing at attention, not daring to move even one muscle. I've stood for as long as two hours at attention.

If you think it's easy, just stand up and try it. Just stand straight with your hands at your sides and look straight in front of you. Don't stand stiffly and don't move anything but your eye lashes. Of course, you don't have any gear. But it isn't easy, is it?

After the inspection is over, the Officer of the Day will leave. If everybody passed the inspection as they did tonight, then all is well and the Cpl. in charge of the first relief will post his guards, thus relieving the man that has had the guard for the last 24 hours.

Tonight I have the second relief. I go on at 8 and off at 12. On again tomorrow morning at 8 and off at 12.

On post, the first thing a sentry learns is what the special orders are. Then he stands at ease; no smoking, no talking to anybody except in the line of duty, no whistling or singing. No sitting down. He must keep on the alert, observe everything taking place within sight or hearing. When I'm on post, my bayonet is fixed and my rifle is fully loaded. If I have trouble I can't handle by myself, all I have to do is let out a yell, "Cpl. of the guard, post #2." Help will arrive after the other guards in between me and the Cpl. have repeated the call. Or, in my case, I just fire a shot in the air. It makes them awfully mad, but it brings help faster than anything else. To heck with 'em. I want to go home. I might have to pay for the round used.

A sentry may call for relief if he gets sick or has to go to the head. He does not under any conditions leave his post until properly relieved.

May the Lord help you if you are caught asleep on guard. Some officers and NCOs are pretty hard on a man when they catch him asleep on guard. In the case of some who were caught, it was forgotten. Others were restricted for 30 days or given five days confinement or bread and water. One case I know of, the boy won't be home for several years. Another case, the boy will never be home. These last two happened while in combat.

What happens when a sentry kills someone while on guard and in line of duty? If I should happen to kill someone while on guard tonight, assuming it's in line of duty, I would be charged with murder and sent before a General Court Martial. I would be found guilty and fined $1 and the cost of the ammo I used. That's the way it's supposed to work. I would be found guilty so the case couldn't be reopened at a later date.

I'm told a formal guard mount is different. I've never stood one. As I understand it, a formal guard is stood in dress blues. Even the finger nails have to be trimmed a certain way. The trouser creases are so sharp you would cut your hands if you should touch them. That's what I'm told.

Although it's the main job of the Marine Corps, I have yet to meet the man who likes guard duty. The Marines have guarded everything from a keg of nails to kings.

The lights just went out all over the city. I got out my flashlight.

Wigal gave me two pictures there were made on Guam I shall enclose. I also was able to acquire a picture of two native girls on Guam.


Nov. 16, 1945. Tsingtao, China. There are ships in the harbor waiting to take some of us home. At the same time, the booming of the big guns can be heard. One regiment dug in on the airfield yesterday. Don't expect me until you see me coming.

I was out on the airfield this morning, and I came in at noon so I could go to air conditioning school. I was met at the door by the Duty NCO and informed I was driving a recon for the afternoon. I made a noise and was told it was regrettable. I was told to get my rifle.  All truck drivers carry their rifles loaded.  I made it hard on them.  Every time I was told to go some place, I didn't know how to get there and they had to look up somebody to send with me to direct the way.  I had a hard time staying on the left side of the road or street.  The people walk in the streets and it is hard to get them out of the way.  I had to almost keep my hand on the horn and then almost push them off the street with the bumper.

Yesterday and the day before they had me washing walls and windows.  I didn't mind that so much.

I guess a guy has to change a little when he sees people die and even gets shot at himself.  Oh, well.

I don't believe there's anything to worry about.  Even if we do get into a few fights over here, I don't believe I'll be in great danger.  I'm hoping I can get to leave before it starts.  I can't see the reason for us being here in the first place.


Nov. 18, 1945.  I'm still here and don't know when I shall be leaving.  As we understand it here, the dock workers won't unload and repair men won't repair ships that aren't slated to bring back service men from overseas.  For the most part, it's expected ships are to transport troops and supplies for other countries that are having trouble with their own.  We all know men still here with 85 or more points, waiting to get home.  As far as I know, there are none in my company with more than 70 points.  They were taken to some little island such as Guam and are still there.  Meanwhile, a number of our ships are transporting Chinese troops from south China and north China.

The sun Is shining and it isn't too cold.  It might get colder tonight.  It always gets colder at night.  We have no way of knowing how cold it gets.  Yesterday morning there was frost all over everything.  I'd say it was getting chilly when it does that.  It's the dampness that goes with the cold that hurts.


Nov. 19, 1945.  I'm still waiting and hoping.  We hear lots of things.  Some of them are that the people back home are applying pressure for us to be taken out of China.  I hope so.  I've seen all of China I want to see.

I had only four hours of guard duty last night.  All day today I've slept and read, something I don't get to do much any more.  It was nice.  My watch was split: two hours last night and two early this morning.  The Officer of the Day caught me both times.  He tried to catch me up, which he did.  But at the same time, I caught him up and corrected him.  The Cpl. of the guard who was with him on his rounds had a hard time holding his sides in.  He came around later and we both laughed together.

This Lt., a new one in the company, is all right, though. He wants to be very G.I., but he goes about it in a way that isn't resentful.

There goes the bugle.  There's a lecture on the G.I. Bill of Rights.  It's a joke.  It can be used of course, but---.  Oh, well, I don't think we will have time to worry about it.  Only half of the company goes at a time.  I don't go tonight.

Nov. 21, 1945. Tsingtao, China.  I was out in a jeep this afternoon. I was sent out along with two S/Sgts and one Sgt. to nail up a couple of signs on a couple of bridges.  Guess who did the work. Nope, you're wrong.  I played with the kids that crowded around. I tried to hit their toes with a hammer while the two staffs and the Sgt., who did most of the work, nailed up the signs.

There are always kids crowding around and begging cigarettes, food, money, etc.  As they crowded around, yelling and putting their hands in the air, I tried to play with them by trying to hit their toes with a hammer.  One boy didn't pull back his toes like the rest did and I almost did hit them.  I looked up; he wasn't laughing like the rest.  He said something to me in a quiet voice which of course I didn't understand.  I figured he was begging for something.  Something in his face, however, told me to leave him alone, that he wasn't to be horsed around with.  I ignored him and played with the rest.  It wasn't long until he was in front of me again.  He didn't stick out his hands and laugh and yell.  He just spoke those same words in a soft, quiet voice.  I turned and asked on of the staffs what he was saying, and he couldn't understand any more than I could.  I started to ask why he didn't throw up his hands and act like the rest, when his coat fell open.  I froze and I know my blood was all in my feet.  I grabbed his arms and pulled them out and took a good look.  His hands had been <u>chopped</u> off just above the wrists.  He was about 8 years old.  He jerked his arms away from me and hid them under the coat again.  I didn't feel like playing any more.  I filled my pipe and lit it.  All the time, he was trying to put those same words over to me.

The Sgt. finished with his job, turned and gave the boy a look.  He, saying that he didn't know what the boy was trying to tell me, put two $100 bills in the little pocket on the coat and said he thought that might help.  When he did that, several Chinese men leaning against a wall not far away clapped their hands and stuck their thumbs in the air and yelled, "very good."  We climbed in the jeep and left.  As we pulled away, we could hear the little boy still yelling those same words.  The words had become a yell only after we had gotten into the jeep.  I suppose I'll spend the next hundred years wondering what it was he was trying to tell me.

Of course, everything I see isn't like that, but it is only the unusual that I can remember when I'm trying to write it down. Lots of things are nice and lots of them are funny.  Some of them are merely interesting, but so many I do remember are hard to write down.  I don't know how to describe them.

Went to a lecture on the G.I. Bill of Rights.  Went with Milke to the show on the roof.  Some film.  I'll be fighting Japs in my sleep again tonight.  Nuts to 'em.  It's an old film, and I doubt it will be shown in Denver again.  I won't name it.  I know some people who should see it.  But then it wouldn't do much good if they did.  I sincerely hope the U.S. never goes to sleep again like it did the last time.  I'm getting sleepy now.  I hope I do sleep when I hit the sack.


Nov. 24, 1945. Tsingtao, China.  They've been keeping me pretty busy.  I just got in.  It's 7:30 P.M.  Yesterday and this morning I was on a carpenter detail.  The first I had been assigned to.  This afternoon I drove Lt. Poppe around the airfield in a jeep.

Tonight I'm duty driver on the recon.  I took two electricians to the Grand Hotel.  They were having trouble with their lights.  The only time the duty driver has to drive is when something comes up out of the way and he has to drive whoever is sent out on the detail.  It can be at any time of the day or night. I get out of guard duty that once anyway.

"Grand Ole Opry" is now on the radio.  Sounds good, except for one thing:  it makes me homesick.  I notice I'm not the only one, however.  Several people yelled "Turn it off" when it first came on.  It's still going, though.


Nov. 28, 1945. Tsingtao, China.  No, I haven't left.  In fact, I expect to be here for some time now.  We've been given the word we needn't expect to leave here before late next spring.  So----don't look for me until you see me coming.  It burns me up, but there isn't anything I can do about it.  Apparently the order came from Gen. Shepard's office and where he gets the orders is something I don't know.  I'm ready to go home as soon as they give the order.


Dec. 1, 1945. Tsingtao, China.  I've got a bad cold.  My eyes are watering so badly I can hardly write.

We had our Thanksgiving dinner last Thursday because the ship with our food on it didn't arrive soon enough for the Thursday before.  It was a very nice dinner.

I've been doing carpenter work down in the equipment compound. We've built a couple of shacks to store gear in. And we made some other things such as tables and chairs.

The division puts out a bulletin every day now and the <u>Stars and Stripes</u> also reaches us from Shanghai, so we get quite a lot of news here now. Besides that, we have the radio we had on Guadalcanal set up here on the stage. The 6th Division has it's own radio station set up here and we can also pick up other stations, such as Korea, Tokyo, Okinawa, Guam, Australia, and believe it or not, the States by short wave. Some of the stations in the States aren't very clear. Oh yes, we can also pick up the Chinese radio. Lot of good it does us, though. The music is all that we can understand---What am I saying?  We can't even understand that.

Ah-le-oooh!  That is what some of the peddlers yell as they walk down the street with their wares. Others have a small gong with a handle they shake a clang out of with each step they take. Their wares are hung from the two ends of long poles, six or eight feet long. They put it on their shoulders to carry the load. These wares can be anything from fire crackers to whole hogs or beef. Peanuts, eggs and liquors are the most common.

Speaking of this music. It sounds like a nightmare or worse. I have seen some of the instruments. Some of them are nightmares just to look at. One trumpet, at least that's what I would call it, was about eight feet long. They have the bass drums and snare drums and the same trumpets that we have. The only thing is they don't sound the same. Of course you understand they have their own names for all of these, but I couldn't remember them even if I tried which I don't. There's one instrument that looks something like a banjo, only it isn't. It has only three strings and sounds like a toy piano. They also have the wooden spoons, only they don't sound like wooden spoons. They sound like somebody hitting a barrel with a hammer.

One instrument looks like a harp, only it's small enough to hold on the lap. With a good player, it sounds good for about five minutes; after that, it's time to take off. Oh yes, they also have the harmonica. Do they know how to play it? I don't know. It isn't the way it sounds when I play it.

I tried to buy one of these three-string banjos, but he wanted $50,000 for it. That sounded a little high to me.

I had a chance to go to a Chinese opera this afternoon, but I didn't feel in the mood with my cold the way it was. Several from this company did go, but I haven't found out what they thought of it.

Down at the equipment compound today one of the

coolies found a can of meat.  He grabbed it and took off.  About 40 coolies were hot on his tail.  It was quite a pile of coolies when they caught up with him.  I don't think any of them got any of the meat because I believe it was all spilled.  No, they didn't do it for fun, but we Marines laughed.  If we looked at it other than funny, we would soon go nuts.  The Americans pay the coolie 23¢ a day, which is more than he ever got before.  Part of that goes for income tax--about 4¢, I believe.

The other day I came out of the mess hall here at the school to wash my mess gear and saw a number of coolies around a G.I. can.  I walked over closer and observed some bones the cooks had thrown out after they had gotten all the meat off they could.  The coolies were chewing them like a dog does.  I almost lost my meal.  The bones were raw.  You'd think there was something we could do about it, but there isn't.  We're having trouble getting enough food for ourselves.  Boy, will I be happy when I can eat a good home-cooked meal.

We can't get stamps.

Dec. 3, 1945. Tsingtao, China.  My cold is much better; in fact, I'm feeling fine.  I'm still doing carpenter work at the compound. I guess we will be kept pretty busy down there for awhile.  We have a welding shop to build and some shipping crates to construct.  The more the better.  It keeps us out of close order drill.  I don't mind the close order drill so much, but they were beginning a lot of fancy stuff I don't go for, such as the marching manual.  It's done in 19 counts while marching with the rifle. Each movement is made in time with the marching.  That's only one of several dozen.  It looks nice when everybody can get it together, but it isn't for me. I'd much rather be doing something else.

The last time I had close order drill, the commanding officer of the engineer battalion came out and watched us go through our stuff and let us all know he liked it and thought it looked wonderful.  Of course that spurred the Lts. and Sgts. on to great deeds.  I thought their buttons were going to snap off their shirts when they snapped to attention.  I figured that was enough for me and started "banging ears" and got myself on this detail. I had a half-dozen men ask for me to be put on their detail before, so it wasn't hard to get on one.

There's only two of us yardbirds on this detail.  There is one Staff, one Sgt., two Cpls., and we two Pfcs.  Who does the work?  Not us two.  We have to be told everything to do and how to do it, etc.  Well, it isn't quite that bad, but we don't have it very hard.  I take very little interest in what is going on around here any more.  To heck with 'em.  I guess I'm just bitter.  So much for that.  I've got to beat my gums every now and then.

I have guard duty tomorrow night and the following day.  I have post #8 again, inside the building.  I'm told it's now an eight hour post: four on, eight off, then four on.  The rest of the twenty-four hours I just stand by in case something happens and the whole guard has to be called out.  Only once have I been called out with the entire guard, and that time not only the entire guard was wakened, but everybody in the area.  That was on Okinawa.  None of us had to fire a shot, but we were in a position to see plenty of hell.

Dec. 5, 1945.  Tsingtao, China.  I've stood my two reliefs and am now standing by until this afternoon when everybody has to fall out for some kind of ceremony.  The pioneers are having theirs right now.  The bugle just sounded the signal that the General is in the area.  In fact, he's now reading something in front of the formation.  Those poor guys have been standing out there for more than an hour waiting for him.   We'll be doing it this afternoon. Some of the boys are getting medals for brave things they did on Okinawa.  It seems as though only a few get them.  There are very few men who didn't earn at least one medal.

It's now after chow and I'm ready for the big event, I hope.   The General decided to go through the barracks this morning.  We did a hurry up job on getting things squared away.  When the Top Sgt. came in and told us he was going through the building, I said he wouldn't come in here.  He didn't.  We were ready and waiting for him when the word came he had left the area.  That's how it goes.

There she blows...well, that's over with.  Four enlisted men and one captain got the bronze star pinned on them by the General.  Two of the enlisted men were from this company.

The ships leaving Shanghai have no Marines on them.  They're all Army.  I'll take that back.  I believe there were a few Marines on one ship that left a couple of weeks ago.  They were not from the 1st or 6th Divisions.

We feel the cold after being in the South Seas.  Our blood is thin and the wind blows and it does freeze here.  I've seen ice on the water several mornings.  As for my longies, I finally realized that was what was causing my skin to feel like a steel brush was going all over it.  I guess I won't wear the longies any more than I have to.

I found out I can get one year of trade training under the G.I. Bill of Rights.  I'd have to leave home to do it, though.

I'm sure I won't be on any ship leaving Shanghai if and when I do get to go home.  All the Marines I know anything about are in or north of Tsingtao.  There are fewer Army men in China than Marines.  In fact, there are about five times as many Marines.

Dec. 7, 1945.  Tsingtao, China.  Our mail is catching up with us. This company alone got 13 big bags today.

We have another inspection tomorrow.  This time we have to stand by our sacks in full greens less the head gear.  The commander of the engineer battalion will inspect.

For the first time since I've been in the Marines, I was put in charge of a detail tonight.  It was left up to me to call the muster for the men who had missed the G.I. Bill of Rights lecture and march them to a make-up lecture.  I did all right.

I was listening to the radio for a report I was told was on this morning's broadcast.  I hope it's a false rumor, but it seems Gen. Gedemeyer gave out the report that all Marines are frozen in China, regardless of points.

The last Marine who left here had 24 months overseas. Anyone with that many months was allowed to go home regardless of the number of points they had.  If I have to stay here another seven months, I guess I'm not going to like it at all.  There is nothing I can do about it though.

Dec. 10, 1945.  Tsingtao, China.  I've been lazy the last two days. I read all day yesterday and part of Saturday.  They are now singing "going home" on the radio for the 60-pointers who they state will be boarding ship soon.  That "soon" is all I've heard since I've been here.  Soon seems to be a long time.

The inspection turned out to be a shake down.  They really pulled a fast one.  We got all cleaned up and put on our greens as called for, and when time came for the inspection, the officers all marched in.  Somebody yelled "Attention!"  Then we were told "At ease."  Then came the order to open all sea bags and locker boxes.  I don't know what it was they were looking for, but they didn't find it on me.  I did have several things I wasn't supposed to have, but nothing was said about them.  Of course pulling it the way they did, nobody had a chance to hide or get rid of anything they weren't supposed to have.  They even looked under the pad on the sack.  I understand a number of men were run up for having things in the sea bags they weren't supposed to have.  One man just two sacks away from me had office hours for having a Jap bayonet in his sea bag.

I'm duty driver on the recon again tonight.  Just in case I haven't told you, a recon is a 1-ton truck, used for light hauling. In this case, it has seats in it for personnel.

The sooner they let me go home the better I'll like it.  I

feel my part of the job is over.  They seem to think they have to have a replacement in advance before they can let anyone leave. How soon those replacements will be in is something nobody knows.

Cover of North China pictorial booklet

Patch of the 6th Marine Division

Pfc Fred T. Klemm, 1st Casual Co., Marine Bks., Treasure Island,
San Francisco, Calif.


Jan. 1, 1946.  Treasure Island.  It's sure good to be back in the
good old States.  We've been told we will be here at least 72
hours.  I'll either go from here to Great Lakes or Camp Pendleton.
I believe it'll be Camp Pendleton.  There I'll receive my discharge
and be on my last lap home.

We left China the 14th.  We were 18 days on the water. I
was put on mess duty the second day out but it wasn't at all bad.
Every other day on duty.  A few days out we hit a storm and of
course I got seasick.  When we crossed the International Date
Line, we went to bed on Sunday and got up on Sunday morning.

We arrived in the harbor here, we were met by a boat with
the words "Welcome Home" painted on each side.  Lots of girls
on the deck.  A loud speaker system let us hear the band they had
on board.  On the stern was a large Christmas tree.  On the
mountain sides and on the sides of the buildings the big words
"WELCOME HOME" and "WELL DONE" could be seen clearly.

We got off on pier #7 and put our sea bags aboard a
truck, got hot coffee and donuts and a Christmas gift from the
Red Cross, and went right aboard a ferry that took us across to
Treasure Island.

We hadn't been on land more than 20 minutes when we
were surrounded by a riot squad armed with shotguns and
submachine guns.  It seems we China Marines are supposed to be
pretty rough and rugged.  As soon as the ten per cent who's
always with us started popping off, the riot squad appeared.  I'm
too near home to get into trouble now.  I had to laugh, though.
The boys must have just got out of boot camp, they were so
scared and shaking so that I thought sure they would drop their
weapons. They didn't stay with us long.  We're just happy, and
not looking for trouble.

We haven't done anything today but eat the biggest chow
at noon that I've put away since I have been in the Corps.  I had
forgotten it was New Year's Day.  I had spent most of the morning
sending the telegram.  I didn't feel very hungry until they started
piling the stuff on my tray. The stuff was heaped up.  I could have
even gotten more.  I got back to the table and looked at it. I'd have
sworn I couldn't eat it all, but I did.  Boy, it was good.

We would have gotten liberty if that ten per cent hadn't
popped off yesterday.  As it is, we can go anywhere on the island,

but no place else.  This is a Navy base and of course it is run by the Navy.  Some of the boys had to yell at every girl they saw, and when the Navy cops called them on it they threw back some wise cracks.  Then when we got to chow, which was as soon as we could get our packs off, something like 14 ranks hit the mess hall door at the same time.  The Navy was expecting only two.  That's when the real trouble started.

I was in the rear and couldn't see or hear what was going on.  The Navy tried to run a jeep through our group to break us up and of course the Marines took hold of it and were going to turn it over.  Then the riot squad arrived.  I eased up through the crowd where I could find out what the scoop was.  One man who had to pop off to the officer in charge of the riot squad was put under arrest.  I thought sure they were going to try taking the guns away from the riot squad.  We could have done it very easily, but then it wouldn't have helped us any.  I don't believe anyone meant any harm.  We were just happy and when the Navy told us to settle down it didn't set right.


Jan. 2, 1946.  Treasure Island.  I'm just fine.  No one bothers us at all.  We can get everything we need right on this island.

I leave tomorrow for Mare Island where I'm supposed to receive my discharge.  Looks like it won't be long now.

Besides Mare Island, wherever that is, men will go to the Marine Corps base in San Diego, Camp Lejeune, Bambridge and Great Lakes.  Men going to the East Coast are drawing clothes here.

They are issuing drawers and socks; I'm to draw mine at Mare Island.  So far nothing has been taken from us.  Looks like I might get to bring my whole sea bag home.  I could use the biggest part of it.  All my combat gear was turned in in China except for my helmet and pack.  Why they had us keep the helmet is something I don't know.  It's only in the way.

They pulled a fast one on us before we left China.  We were told we were leaving at a certain time, to pack up and be ready.  When the time came, we had a shake down.  We stayed until the next day.  How did I know they wouldn't be pulling that stuff for a week or more?  They took a wool shirt off of me.  Don't worry, it's all right.  I've a lotta stuff I'm not supposed to have. So has most every other man.


Jan. 4, 1946.  Mare Island.  This will be the last place I will go before I get my discharge, so they tell us.  I'm to receive my discharge on Thursday, Jan. 10th.  If everything goes right, I should be in Denver a week from Sunday.

On Thursday, I'll send my sea bag COD. I understand I'll be allowed 5¢ per mile for my ticket. I pay for the ticket out of that. According to some other fellows here, they were only paid 1½¢ per mile. How about that?

They won't pay us until the last day when they give us our discharge. I still have $10 so I'll get by. As I figure it, I'll get close to $200.

We arrived here yesterday but they didn't have room for us in "Guadalcanal Village," so we were taken to the main barracks where everything was messed up. We did get a bed for the night, however, and today we're in "Guadalcanal Village." It is just what the name implies. We almost have to have a row boat to get in and out. We can take it for a few days, though. The chow is plenty good. Even the air is different from overseas.

While I think of it, Mare Island is some twenty-odd miles from Treasure Island north of San Francisco, Treasure Island is the same place where they had the World's Fair. It's a man-made island.

Jan. 9, 1946. Mare Island. I'm due in Denver at 2 P.M. Saturday afternoon. I'm due to leave the Oakland pier at 7:30 Thursday evening. I'll receive close to $70 for the trip. My ticket will cost me something like $20. There are two pieces of paper I have to have, and I have one already. The other I get tomorrow.

It won't be long now.

(Arrived Denver Jan. 12, 1946 at about 10 A.M.)

Christmas card, 1945

Part II: Korean War

<u>Introduction</u>

Korea was divided at the 38th parallel at the end of World War II, with the Soviet Union taking control of the northern section and the United States taking the southern section. The defeated Japanese, who had ruled Korea since 1910, surrendered. The United Nations General Assembly called for UN-supervised elections throughout Korea in 1947. Elections were held in the U.S.-occupied zone, but not in the north. In 1948, The Republic of Korea (ROK) was established in the south, and the Democratic People's Republic of Korea (DPRK) was established by the Soviet Union in the North. The leader of North Korea, Kim Il Sung, claimed authority over all of Korea, but the UN General Assembly declared the ROK to be the only lawful government in Korea. The United States withdrew its military forces in 1949. On June 25, 1950, North Korean forces invaded the Republic of Korea.

The United Nations engaged in its first collective action through the establishment of the UN Command, led by Gen. Douglas MacArthur, U.S. Army. Eventually, 16 member nations sent troops and assistance.[1] Initially, American Army troops on occupation duty in Japan were sent to Korea to halt the invasion. These troops were not trained for combat, and they did not have the equipment they needed. They were pushed into the tip of Korea at Pusan. Gen. MacArthur called for more troops, including U.S. Marines. The request for Marines came on 2 July, and the 1st Provisional Brigade sailed from San Diego on 12 July.

The Marines, and other military forces, had been cut after World War II. In order to meet combat needs, the Organized Reserve was mobilized.[2] All across the country, ceremonies were held at bus stations and train depots as Marine Reservists were shipped out. At Denver's Union Station, Governor Walter Johnson and various military leaders gave speeches, and the band from Lowry Air Force Base played military music.[3]

One of the Denver reservists was Cpl. Fred T. Klemm. After World War II, he had been promoted to Cpl. and discharged. He returned to his job with the Denver Public Schools. In February of 1950, he joined the Reserves. The recruiter said: "We need you experienced men to train the new ones, and it's only one weekend a month. Think of the extra money!" His wife and two daughters, ages 8 and 10, were devastated when he was called up and shipped overseas. His letters home show that he tried very hard to not make them worry; he tried to find things to write about other than combat.

94

## Chapter 1: The Trip Across

I was called to active duty Aug. 1, 1950, and left Denver Aug. 2nd. Bob Wilson [another employee of the Denver Public Schools] left at the same time. We arrived at Camp Pendleton at 4 A.M. Aug. 5th. On Aug. 6th, I was assigned to motor transport: 1st MT Bn., 1st Marine Division as a driver. Lily [Jackson, sister] and her family visited me. Aug. 7th: assigned to auto maintenance company. Met Bob Coni, also from Denver.

Aug. 8th and 9th: loaded a ship in San Diego.

Aug. 10th: 1st Lt. Bob Wilson was assigned to special service, headquarters. Bob was a teacher at South High School.

Aug. 12, 1950 marked a 12-hour shift. Many men are as old as I am (33). Received $22.05 reserve pay and $20 regular pay. Received my 782 gear: rifle, pack, etc.

Aug. 13, 1950. The ship we are loading is the African Patriot; it flies the Union Jack. I haven't stood an inspection yet; haven't heard a bugle. Duty NCO turns out the light at 10 P.M. and on again at 5:30 A.M. I'm aware of many changes since World War II.

Aug. 20, 1950. Boarded General Meigs, a dirty ship. Sailed from San Diego Aug. 18th. It was announced that we were headed for Yokohama, Japan. It was the first time I ever saw a doctor go into the holds and check the men lying in the bunks. Many were seasick. We had rifle inspection and instruction. Coni sticks to me like glue; he thinks we should stick together. The ship is crowded. Movies are shown on deck. We have abandon ship drills every day. My bunk is on the bottom deck. If they could've gotten us any lower, I'm sure they would have.

Aug. 23, 1950. May get carpenter assignment; hope I don't get driver assignment. Sat around most of the day and read, smoked my pipe, and played my harmonica.

Today is Thursday, Aug. 24, 1950. Tomorrow we cross the International Date Line and it will be Saturday, Aug. 26, 1950. I watched two movies, one on the deck and one through a porthole in the officers' lounge. I liked the one in the lounge best; it was a western. Some of the men said they saw a whale, but I didn't see it.

We each have two of the nicest white wool blankets I have ever seen.

Aug. 27, 1950. We have changed course. We are to go to Kobe, Japan instead of Yokohama. The water is rough and choppy and the men are getting restless. It's hot in the compartment. Inspection.

Aug. 28, 1950. School on machine guns. I have a crew cut. I'm wondering if the mail is to be censored. The officers don't think so.

Aug. 30, 1950. The water is as smooth as glass. We expect to arrive tomorrow even though we haven't seen land.

Aug. 31, 1950. Master-Sgt. Johnson approached me and announced he expected to put me to work as soon as we're ashore. It seems he needs a carpenter.

Sept. 2, 1950. Kobe, Japan. Docked yesterday. Gear and equipment are being unloaded. It's hot, crowded, mucky, and we had exercises on the top deck in the rain. The food is terrible. So far no work assignment. Some men worked all night last night.

I received 16 cards and letters. Some men are getting liberty. I would like to see what the town is like and see if I can get some pipe tobacco.

After lunch--I have a chair and my feet are up on the rail. Just one great adventure for me so far. I was hoping I could send something home, but have only $7. My clothes and gear are damp and smelly and I need to get where I can do some washing. I'm watching some giant cranes unload another ship across the pier. Jap coolies are doing most of the unloading. They are all over the ship here. We have guards on our personal gear and guards are walking the docks also. The Army supervises everything.

The 15th Army band was on the pier playing the Marine Hymn as we docked. They played some other pieces before they left. Some of the Denver men arrived last Tuesday, having come across on another ship. They are quartered in barracks. They came aboard for a visit.

Sept. 4, 1950. Kobe, Japan. Sun is shining, weather nice. Rain and wind yesterday. [Typhoon.][4] More fun. They tried to get us ashore, but only a few made it. The moorings broke loose and we found ourselves using the pads from our bunks to brace ourselves against the bulkheads the best we could so as not to get thrown against them and get our few brains bashed out. Only once before had I heard the alarm sound and really mean it. Adventure, thrills, we have everything.

My first assignment was Duty NCO. Nothing to it. Checked the men out and in on liberty. Eleven came in late. I would have checked them all in on time, but the Top Sgt. came around at the time they were due. So now I'm in the dog house with the men. Today is Labor Day. My company got paid $20 each while I was on NCO duty.

Sept. 5, 1950. Kobe, Japan. Received driver's permit this morning. Still don't have dog tags. Lt. Wilson told me he understood the wind got up to 120 miles per hour last Sunday, the worst since 1934.

The ship I went from Guadalcanal to Okinawa on is along side of us [U.S.S. Caymer.][5] Am running out of pipe tobacco; there are no cigarettes either.

Sept. 7, 1950 Kobe, Japan. Got paid $20 yesterday, occupation money. Mr. Truman lost some votes. Some of the men are pretty sore. We got it from the <u>Stars and Stripes</u> first. [Occupation money was worthless to send home, and there wasn't much to spend it on in Japan.][6] Got shots yesterday also. Hurt rather badly. I was put in charge of a detail yesterday morning, and a little later taken off of it and put on guard duty. For four hours I kept anyone from smoking on the docks while gasoline was being loaded.

Klemm family, Aug. 1950

Chapter 2:  Inchon and Seoul

Sept. 18, 1950.  Inchon, Korea.  Stood at the rail of the General Jackson PA 18 and watched the first wave go into Inchon.  [The start of the invasion, behind enemy lines.][7]  Have lived 33 days aboard.  It'll be good to get my feet on solid ground again.  At present am waiting orders to go ashore.  Haven't fired my rifle yet.  Don't know if I will.  We were in another storm at sea.  Got very sick although seasick pills helped some.

Have pipe tobacco again.  Understand we are to get two free beers when we go ashore.  Expect to keep pretty busy, though.


Sept. 20, 1950.  Inchon.  Seven weeks since I left Denver.  It seems like years.  We are about 15 miles from the front lines.  As I understand it, we are now living in what once was Jap barracks and then the U.S. Army had it.  We are on the second floor of a concrete building.  The shops are down below and in a second building nearby.  Windows are almost all broken out.  I think I'll fare pretty well.  I have a cot, sleeping bag, two blankets, and a field jacket.

I'm sure my pack weighed more than 100 pounds when I came down the net on the side of the ship.  It was a full transport pack with everything except my cot on it, plus my M1 rifle.  Some wise guy told me to get the lead out, and another wise-acre said to leave the old man alone.

I haven't received an assignment.  There is no need for a carpenter.  I followed MSgt. Johnson and then SSgt. Heninger around and got myself assigned to a machine shop.  He has four mobile machine shops.  I don't know anything about the work, but I can learn.

They are expecting a break through the lines.


Sept. 23, 1950.  Inchon.  Received tobacco in the mail.  Another pack was handed to me by a man I didn't even know. The other man in the machine shop is a Sgt. and he seems to know his business.  There is talk about being too far behind the lines.  One of the staff just took several men around me for a detail.  I didn't look up and he by-passed me.  I received the clippings in the mail, and they caused a great deal of excitement.

I had one of the natives wash my clothes today.  He charged me one pack of cigarettes, which I got from Coni.  Coni was assigned to mechanic, working on 6x6 trucks.  In Denver, he was a driver's license examiner.  I can see all the trucks that come in from where I work in the machine shop.  One a tank ran into, one was shelled and turned over, one is full of machine gun bullets. There are jeeps, too. Some Army trucks and jeeps are in here too. I noticed some flashes and heard some big booms last night.

I understand the mighty U.N. is now helping us. The English I have seen. One of their destroyers came along as escort for us.

The South Koreans are all over the place--none of us can tell the difference between them and the North Koreans.

The Marines have one password and the Army another. The South Koreans have still another. I can't figure out who is supposed to keep from shooting who. I don't have the wanderlust, so stay pretty close to where I belong.

Aboard the PA 18 (Gen. Jackson), we were hit by a typhoon. First the ship would go one way, then the other. In the mess hall the tables, benches, men, food and everything else that wasn't tied down would slide from one side to the other. When the ship went to the other side, everything slid back again, and the bulkhead or wall stopped it. I had just gotten my tray filled and was on my way to a table when the first blow came. I slid on my feet down an aisle with my tray in one hand and my coffee cup in the other until I came to a post. I wrapped myself around it and hung on. I didn't spill a drop. The second time it happened, I had just finished eating. After that, they tied the tables up against the wall or bulkhead and we sat with our trays on the floor or deck.

Here on the second floor of this concrete building, there are perhaps 300 men in one large room. There was fire at the bottom of the stairs. (Some oily rags, trash, and such.) Some of the men calmly went about putting the fire out while others grabbed their rifles, cartridge belts, helmets, and left the building. Still some others picked up their gear and equipment and threw the whole business out the window. After the fire was out, they had to go out in the dark and find their stuff.

South Koreans will be allowed to enter Seoul first and repair their capital.

PX supplies are brought in and distributed free: poggypate (candy), pipe tobacco, cigarettes, etc.


Sept. 24, 1950. Inchon, on the way to Seoul. Ran the lathe in the machine shop for the first time.

A guitar and harmonica are being played.
Sept. 24, 1950. Coni went to hospital with piece of steel in his eye.

I have plenty of pipe tobacco now. They often pass it out free. Men who don't smoke pass their allotment on to me.

Sept. 26, 1950.  Haven't seen any beer yet.  A can a day wouldn't hurt anyone.

Sept. 26., 1950.  A silk factory near Seoul.  Can see planes diving on Seoul.  This is a funny war.  I haven't done enough work to pay for my meals.  My machine shop is outside the factory building while one is inside.  We are to take turns at it.

I went ashore at Inchon on the LST 883; drove a truck off in the dead of night without lights.

SSgt. Heninger is saying that all Marines and most Army will be out of Korea by the 15th of next month and everyone will be home for Xmas.  I'm not counting on it till it happens.

There are lots of mud huts with straw roofs.  Many Koreans follow along with us; they work in the mess hall, shops, and do laundry.  One man wants us to hurry and get into Seoul so he can find his wife and kids.  It hasn't rained since I came ashore and the dust is terrible.

Sept. 30, 1950.  I learned how to use the valve grinder.  There's lots of work for the machine shop now.  It's getting colder.  They issued sweaters.

Oct. 1, 1950.  Moved through Seoul yesterday.  (The town with the silk factory is Yongdungpo.)  Am working as carpenter today, building crates.  Coni is back; his eye is all right.

Col. Beall talked this morning.  If the U.N. said for us to move across the 38th parallel, we would.  If they said "no," we would be California bound.  Cold weather clothing is being issued. Maj. Roberts, our company commander, said he didn't know, but felt plans called for us to practice-land in Alaska.  There's lots of scuttlebutt.

While moving yesterday, I saw thousands of Koreans as they moved with their few belongings back to their homes in Seoul.  There is no electric power, no telephones, no water, nothing but ruble.  We had to lift trolley wires over our loaded trucks.  Trolleys sat in the middle of the streets.  All through the city of ruin were signs--"Welcome U.N. Police," "Welcome U.N. Forces," "Welcome U.S. Marines," "Welcome U.S. Army," "We are glad to be friends with you."  I noticed one thing outstanding: white clothes that came to the ground were clean, starched, and ironed.  These people love white.  The dust raised by our trucks and equipment didn't leave them white for long.  Already the people have started rebuilding, filling in shell holes in the streets, etc.

We are living in a wooden structure that must have once

been a stable. It has a wooden floor that shakes when someone walks across it. Someone is always walking across it. There couldn't be a better fire trap for 250 men to be living in.

The company is being rearranged into combat platoons. I'll remain assigned to the machine shop, except when they need a carpenter. Understand they are to pay us again. Wonder what for--there's no place to spend it. One of the office clerks told me my name was on the promotion list. I'll keep my fingers crossed.

Oct. 3, 1950. Seoul. Was paid $20 in occupation money yesterday. Understand Gen. Carter, the commandant, was in the area a short while back.

Got through with carpenter work today, building crates and boxes. May work in the machine shop tonight. I was assigned to the 2nd squad, 2nd platoon. (Repair platoon.) One machine shop is to go with each platoon and each platoon is assigned to a letter company. We still don't know where or when we are going.

We have a bugle now. It was played for the first time today to the cheers of the men.

We were issued our first beer this evening, one can per man @15¢. We have electric lights in the old barn now. Someone found a radio.

A little Korean boy had us in circles last night. He drew the outlines of the different countries of the world, named each, and its most important product. In many cases, we couldn't agree with him because we didn't know. He had many questions we couldn't answer. I'm proud to say I knew more of them than anyone else in the group. He named cities, their population and whether or not they were capitals, etc.

Oct. 5, 1950. Seoul. A show at Division Headquarters tonight. Helmet, cartridge belt and rifle required. Some kind of stage show and I don't think it is worth the trouble.

Sgt. Pareder, the man I work with in the machine shop, received a radiogram last night. He's the proud papa of a baby girl born Sept. 27.

Oct. 8, 1950. Inchon. We're on the move, preparing to board ship. We don't know where we're going. Don't think we're heading home. In the machine shop, we're trying to look busy so as not to get put on some work detail.

We cleaned all the tools and equipment as we were told to do. We keep a rag handy and if someone comes around, we wipe off the oil we put on the tools and put some more on. Most everyone thinks we are headed for home. I don't think so.

Oct. 9, 1950. Inchon. Received package in mail call, put it under my arm and went over and drew winter underwear. When I opened the package later in my tent, more winter longies.

Cpl. of the Guard tonight for the first time. Lt. Wilson is Officer of the Day.

Oct. 13, 1950. Inchon. I was informed my M.O.S. [Military Occupation Specialty] was changed to 1331 machinist. Looks like they maybe are satisfied with my work in the machine shop. Tuesday we had our first rain since we arrived here. One shower since. Don't know where we are going. Sounds very much like North Korea. If we don't go above the 38th parallel, which has been approved, I'm sure we will go to Japan.

We didn't see the Bob Hope show. Those shows seldom come to the Marine camps in the field, I don't know why. When they come to an Army camp nearby, we are sometimes permitted to attend. That's providing the Army doesn't object and the Marines obey all the rules, which is hard to do when you don't know them. Army M.P.s watch the Marines very closely and arrest them for the least infraction.

We received beer three days in a row after the first on Oct. 3rd. Haven't seen any since. The Col. put a case of Coke out in the middle of the shop area and walked away. I was one of the first to get to it even though I was the farthest away. For once I kept my mouth shut and ran.

Lt. Wilson didn't bother us the other night while on guard duty. The Col. brought over his personal Korean interpreter about 2:30 A.M. We took a Marine out of the brig who was in for five days bread and water, and put the Korean in. It seems they found out he was a Red spy. The Korean had been sleeping in the same officers' tent with Lt. Wilson and a Captain. Both officers turned white when informed of the incident. The Korean could have cut their throats.

I have been issued a kapoc sleeping bag which is very warm.

Oct. 16, 1950. Inchon. Aboard the Marine Phoenix in harbor. We don't know where we're going, but it sounds like above the 38th. If they are going to get us home by Xmas, they're going to have to hurry. Some are taking bets on when and where we're going. There are many stories.

This is a nice ship and the chow is good. They have real butter on the tables and we can have all we want. Had to take a salt water shower last night, though. I wasn't chosen for mess duty or guard duty, so maybe this will be a good trip, wherever we are going. One thing bothers me. They didn't take up the ammo and each man is loaded down with the stuff.

While loading equipment in hold #5, where I have the top of four bunks, a Jap was pulling on a rope to put some equipment where he wanted it. He lost his footing and fell four decks, the approximate of four stories. The steel at the bottom didn't give.

They let us come up the gang plank when we came aboard. It was a good thing. I wasn't the only one who needed help. We were pretty well loaded down. I left some of my gear in the machine shop which the others couldn't do. Sgt. Pareder and I are the only two who have keys to it.

Mobile machine shop, Korea. Photo courtesy of <u>Leatherneck</u> magazine

Oct. 23, 1950.  Aboard the Marine Phoenix.  Today is Monday. Just a week ago yesterday, we boarded ship.  For six days now, we have done nothing but sail in circles.  [The Navy was clearing mines from the harbor.][8]  We are supposed to be going to Wonsan, North Korea.  It's on the east coast.  I had thought sure we would go to Japan.  We were informed mail would go off the ship at 1300.  The more I think about it, the more I think this is the ship that went nowhere.  Now there is a good title for a story, "The Ship That Went Nowhere."  It could be all about the men aboard and what they left behind when they boarded:  their families, friends, jobs, plans, ideals; and for what?

There had been very little doing aboard ship.  I was put on guard duty last Friday.  I walk post from 12 to 4 during the day and again at night, every other day.  In other words, 24 on and 24 off with eight hours out of the 24 walking post.  Stationed starboard side of the boat deck.  It was windy and cold out there last night. There are several Cpls. walking post.  I don't like guard duty, but it gives me something to do.  There have been no classes or rifle inspections, just a roll call at 10 each morning.  The rest of the time we're on our own.  The food is very good, except that the butter changed to oleo.  We can have all we want to eat.  It's been the best food I've seen since I was called to active duty.  I'm sure I've gained weight.  We line up in the chow line by the numbers.  My number will soon be called.  Those of us who have the 12 to 4 guard are allowed to sleep in.  Of all the ships I have been on, this is the cleanest and best all around.

Oct. 28, 1950.  Wonsan, Korea.  We landed the day before yesterday and got out.  I don't know what we are supposed to be doing here.  I was sure we would be going to Japan, but I was wrong. Very little of our equipment has come in.

I got very sick the night after we landed.  The corpsman worked on me and even the Col. himself crawled into the pup tent with me.  I don't know how he found out about it, but he was going to bring me one of his blankets.  I had all the clothes I owned on, was inside the feather sleeping bag, with two blankets, but I still couldn't get warm.  My head was so hot, however, the corpsman couldn't hold his hand on it.  They talked about taking me back to the ship but they were afraid I'd get wet again.  I'm not the only one sick, but the others don't seem quite as bad.  I feel good enough now, but a little weak.  I was warm and slept good last night.

Our pup tents are on the beach with the airfield on the other side.

I traded one of my cigarette lighters for a jet. It throws out a flame like a small blow torch. Sure nice to light a pipe with. I have fun with it.

Maj. Roberts called a general assembly and passed out some dope. He named some towns, but I can't pronounce them let alone spell them. The repair platoons are to be spread out between here and the Manchurian border. One platoon (he didn't say which) would be right on the border. More cold weather clothing is being issued.

The Major informed me the chief corpsman had told him I had intestinal flu.

It looks as though we're going to be here for awhile. They told us the Army doesn't want us here. Mail is going to be hard to send and receive. I'm now more confused than ever. This is a funny war. I heard one of the officers say there was nothing in the book about a war like this.

The planes are pretty close when they take off and land. One of the runways starts at the end of our row of tents. I still say the ship went nowhere.

I was put on guard duty on top of a stack of rations with direct orders to shoot anyone who came within 100 feet. They forgot about me. I was on top of that stack all night and most of the following day without any type of relief. No one would come close enough for me to send a message to the command. Although I had a parka, it got mighty cold up there. It also rained.

Oct. 29, 1950. Wonsan. They are going to issue parkas. The 1st platoon left this morning. We may move tomorrow.

Oct. 31, 1950. Wonsan. Don't know when we will move. Mail has stopped. We're pretty busy. Have a hard time cleaning up. Living in a big storage tent now. It is dry and warmer but crowded. We were issued parkas, gloves, boots, etc. Where to carry them? News here very confusing. Have radio in the machine shop. The news we got last night didn't sound good.

Nov. 2, 1950. Wonsan. There's lots of rumors. One has it we'll be home for Christmas, but at the same time we're moving inland. My machine shop is the only one left here now, and we expect to get the order to move closer to the border at any time. The place we're supposed to be moving to is called Hamhung.

Some of the fellows have made up a song, "Way down yonder in Yongdungpo where I met her---" and some other words

I didn't try to remember.

Have seen only a few North Korean men. No women yet. Of course I haven't been in any town yet. Neither the South nor North Korean people seem to care too much who rules them. They appear to take for granted whatever government is in command, they will get kicked around anyway.

Nov. 3, 1950. Wonsan. We have lights in our tents now. The 2nd platoon is all that is left of the company now. Everyone has moved inland. I don't know how soon we will also be moving. I sure don't see how we can be home for Xmas when we are moving inland.

The first and second squads are boarding a truck to go to a movie at the airfield. I'm in the 2nd squad, but would rather stay here.

There's eight of us in this storage tent, nothing but Cpls., Pfcs., and Pvts. Most are Cpls. The Sgts., staff and officers each have tents to themselves. Theirs are pyramid tents and they have stoves to heat them with. That's the biggest thing I don't like about military life--no equality. However, I don't mind the storage tent and the stove would have to be taken care of and it might over-heat the tent, and then when we did go outside we would only be much colder--or do I make sense? No, I guess not. Oh--well--anyway, I have a field jacket--a little dirty, but warm, and then there is the parka they issued, which I haven't worn yet, but expect to on guard duty the day after tomorrow night when it will be the 2nd squad's turn. The 4th squad has it tonight. Each man stands a three hour watch, two men at a time. Of course, if we should get attacked, we are all out there in a hurry. We have been alerted twice the last two nights. It seems some of those dopes are sniping in the hills not far away. With almost everyone gone from here it would be--oh! Why worry about it? I have 88 rounds of ammo in my belt. We are issued 48 rounds--I picked up the rest just to have my belt full. When I did that, I was thinking of Okinawa. So far I haven't even seen a tin can I could shoot at.

The chow is good. At present we are eating with the Combat Service Group-Ordinance Unit.

Nov. 6, 1950. Wonsan. This is the fourth night we have been here on our own. Last night I shaved, took a bath, and washed some clothes. We still haven't gotten any mail. I'm sure there's some for us with the company. I wish they'd send it down to us. Because of road conditions, it takes about seven hours to drive the short distance.

The combat service group, as I understand it, has taken

the place of the combat engineers and pioneers that we had during World War II. There are some engineers though. We were in their compound yesterday and picked up some oxygen and gas for welding. They have some nice equipment such as truck cranes. The only ones I saw before were the ones the Army had.

We guys got together and made us an oil stove out of a 55-gallon drum and some odds and ends. It works, too. I think all the tents have stoves now. Anyway, I made several parts in the machine shop that were the same thing and for the same purpose.

We don't get much news here, but according to what we have gotten, the Chinese Reds have moved 41,000 troops to within 20 miles of Hamhung where the rest of our unit is supposed to be. The division command is supposed to be there also.

The men from our unit who were aboard the hospital ship have been coming back. They stay overnight with us and then go on up forward the next morning. The trouble is, the trucks don't come back. One group came in yesterday and is still with us tonight. Maybe when a truck does come back, it will bring our mail.

I have a little gas stove. It is pretty nice. It was brand new when I got it. The only trouble is, I'm afraid to use it for fear someone will see it and take it from me. So far I've been able to carry it with me by rolling it inside my sleeping bag. I obtained it in Inchon. I also obtained a folding camp chair while in Seoul. I've left it in the machine shop for transport. I have it in the tent during the day and so far it hasn't stuck to anybody.

My clothes won't dry. I had them hanging in the tent last night. This morning I hung them outside, and they're still not dry, at 6 P.M. I don't know whether to bring them in or take a chance on losing them. The wind is blowing now, which it seems to do every night.

I've got some more ideas for my basement shop. You know how my ideas work, of course. I look at the catalog, then I wish for a while, then I look at the price and my wishing turns into a dream. In time, I wake up and forget all about it. If I bought all the tools I think I need in the basement, but would only use maybe once in five years, there wouldn't be any money for anything else. I've run and worked with some tools I didn't know existed. For example, a PortoPower. I won't buy one--I'd rather have a new car. I understand the machine shop, fully equipped cost $20,000. A lotta money to put on four wheels and tell a guy like me to go to work in it. I was cutting down the commutator on an armature when a fuse blew out.

The password tonight is Fibber Magee.

Nov. 9, 1950.  Wonsan.  Almost 8 A.M. and we're waiting for work call.  We have everything fixed up here now so we can live half-way comfortable, so it shouldn't be long before we get the order to move.

There's three of us working in the machine shop.  There isn't room inside for three, so yours truly is the one normally pushed out.  I go stand by the fire until one of the officers or staff NCOs assign me to some work.

Looks like they could send a jeep down with our mail.

An Army unit has moved in next door to us.  According to them, they're supposed to take over our ammo dump.  Heard also 1600 Marine replacements came in day before yesterday.  The Combat Service Group got some of them.

Nov. 11, 1950.  Wonsan.  Still no mail and we were supposed to get paid yesterday.  I have a feeling we will soon receive the order to move up with the company.  Even though we've been kept busy, I don't know why we were left behind.

Just had some hot chocolate, heated on my little camp stove.  Wonder if I'll be able to take it home with me when I go.  Doubt it.

The Sgts. have one of the two radios we had in the machine shop.  Neither one would work.  One of the Sgts. took them both some place for repair.  They got one back and have it in their tent. I'm supposed to get the other one when it's repaired.  They invited me over to their tent to listen to the one they have.  According to the news, there are still things happening in Korea.

Nov. 14, 1950.  Wonsan.  We don't have a thermometer, so don't know how cold it is, but when we have to thaw out the water tank to get water, when we throw water out and it freezes as soon as it hits the ground, and when my canteen freezes hanging on the corner of my cot, I think we're having some cold weather.  One of the fellows said, "It isn't cold--it's in our minds," while he wrapped up tighter.  [The temperature was recorded at 20 below zero during the Chosin campaign, not counting wind chill.][9]

We were told there are no plans to move us from here, and we will receive mail Thursday, providing the company gets any.  It appears the company hasn't received any in six days.  Anyway, today we started packing to move.  The lights are going on and off.  Writing by flashlight.  One of the guys just let out a howl--he had crawled into his sleeping bag.  It's like crawling in between two cakes of ice until it warms up.  The lights keep going

108

on and off.  We aren't having any trouble, just a lot of clean fun. I have an idea the nice clean language can be heard in Denver.

The wind is blowing rather hard.  It blew down the shed the mechanics built to work in and dumped it on top of the machine shop and generator.  A few times we expected our tents to go, but so far they've held.

Nov. 17, 1950.  Hamhung.  Writing by candle light.  We got moved up here yesterday over a road I'm sure the devil himself built.  My bottom is still sore tonight.  We spent the day putting up tents and getting squared away, only to be told we would start moving again tomorrow.

Coni is on his way home because of stomach ulcers. They'll keep him in a hospital somewhere for awhile and then send him home.  Several men left who have four or more dependents. One left because of some kind of hardship at home.

The whole thing is very confusing.  The story now is, the Navy is standing by to take us out, but the Army won't let us go. We are supposed to stay here somewhere for the winter.  Unless I get out for having three dependents, I won't be home for Xmas. I received a $100 check this afternoon, and I'll send it home.  A Sgt. just came in who says he heard something that is causing him to take all bets.  He's betting we'll be home for Xmas--this year. We'll have to leave right away if we do.  We're supposed to move across town tomorrow.  The 10th Army is taking over this area.

I'm so dirty I don't think I'll ever get cleaned up again.  I need a shower and a shave.  That'll be nice by candlelight.

I received my dog tags the day after we left Kobe, Japan. They are Army type, made up by the Army in Kobe.

I'm tired and I've never been more confused in my life. I'm going to go nuts yet.  Some sparks just burned a hole in our tent. Sgt. Tucker is trying to wire an electric light in here now.  I got permission to do it, but changed my mind when I heard we were moving tomorrow.  There are nine of us in a pyramid tent. It's too crowded.

Nov. 19, 1950.  Hamhung.  We got moved again yesterday. Worked all day after having guard duty last night.  May move again soon. Everything is very confusing.

They boys are trying to read the <u>Denver Posts</u> I received before lights out.  Sgt. Tucker is frying some bacon on the stove we fixed up.  He's toasting bread and putting bacon in between. Tastes pretty good.  We couldn't fix up an oil burner this time so we are using wood which has to be chopped up.

Sgt. Tucker is a new daddy.  A boy, his first child.  He

refuses to live with the Sgts. in their tent.  He's a pretty good guy so we put up with him.  Anyway, he's our squad leader.  He's 24 or 25 years old.  I'm the oldest in the tent and the youngest is 17.  They call me Pappy.

Nov. 21, 1950.  Hamhung.  We're moving again this morning.  We don't know where we are going, but supposedly 30 miles closer to the boarder.  In addition to moving, we also have the guard tonight.  I have a post for only two hours, 3:30 A.M. to 5:30 A.M.  But I don't have to like it.

The trip from Wonsan to Hamhung took nine and a half hours. Seventy-five miles of road that I'm sure the devil himself built.  We lost two parts trailers.  One we got back on the road but the other one was lost for good.  Several thousand dollars in new parts were lost.  I thought the machine shop would go.  I wasn't worried about the machine shop, but all my gear except for my rifle was in there.  This time my pack and sleeping bag go with me.  This road reminded me of the one-way roads in the Rockies, only this one was a lot rougher.  My sitting down place is still sore. Judging by the stories we get here, we'll be in Korea for some time.  I'm sure I won't make it home for Xmas.  I haven't heard anything about a point system being in use.  I'm sure I have more than 53 points.  All the men with four or more dependents have left and we have replacements for them.  I heard today of more replacements coming in.

There have been no more promotions that I know of.  I'm not trying to get one and I'm not trying to be anybody's hero.  I try to do what they tell me to do and leave it go at that.  I can't feel I'm any longer needed here.  In fact, I can't feel anyone is needed here anymore.  If they want to keep an occupation force here, it's an Army job, not a Marine one.

It's warmer here for the present.  I went without my jacket this afternoon and felt fine.  I wasn't wearing my longies, either.

Nov. 23, 1950.  We're now near a rail head 30 miles from Hamhung.  We're supposed to be about the same distance from the Chosin Reservoir.  We moved up here yesterday and set up camp on a knoll in the middle of a valley.  We had to use metal spikes to tie down our tents; the wooden pegs wouldn't drive into the frozen earth.  We ran wires from the generator in the machine shop and had lights in our tents as well as the area around them.  We were allowed to use flashlights outside the tents and we were allowed to smoke.  We were told to dig fox holes near our tents, but the frozen ground wouldn't yield to our efforts.  A hole was blasted for the Major's radio.  During the afternoon, Army and

Marine trucks brought in beer. Both Army and Marine officers came in jeeps and brought radios and instruments of various kinds. We were told there would be no taps this evening. We were to have all the lights on and the radios were to be turned on top volume.

Sgt. Tucker and I were the only ones to realize we were being used as decoy. Infantry units, special weapons, tanks, etc., moved in around us at dusk. They had no fires, lights, and there was no smoking. They dug in and aimed their guns at a gap between two ranges of hills. Tuck and I checked our rifles and carried them with us. We didn't say anything to the other men for fear they would panic. Some of them were already pretty happy as a result of the beer they had drunk.

No guard was assigned. None was posted. I took it on myself to walk around the tents. I found one man lying next to an oil heater; his parka was smoking. I pulled him away.

I felt many eyes watching me as I walked under the lights. The Major, who was the only officer with us, came to me and said he wanted me to kill the generator when the firing started.

Shortly after 1 A.M., all hell broke loose. A mortar was fired not more than five paces from me in some shrubs. I had no idea it was there. I raced for the machine shop and was turning off the generator when I heard the Major yell, "Clem, kill the generator." Without a generator, there were no radios or lights. I stood in the darkness and watched as the gap became a firey hell with the guns all around me firing into it. Jet planes firing rockets made dive after dive.

As the night broke into day, everything became quiet. As the sun rose and reflected on the snow, I started to walk up to the gap. On the trail I was following, I met two fellows from the Infantry coming down. They said they could only count heads and had become sick at the sight. I turned and followed them back. No one in the two platoons used as a decoy had been hurt.

We had chow at 3:30 today. Turkey with all the trimmings, dressing, cranberry sauce, potatoes, fruit cake, nuts, candy, bread, coffee. Well, there were 16 different things served, and all we wanted. I can't remember what they were all called. It was very good and we are rather happy tonight.

It's raining and cold. I'm sure it will turn to snow by morning. We now have a regular oil stove for our tent and also a wood deck or floor. There are still nine of us in this tent. Over each sack on the tent is written the name of the man's home state.

Received a letter from the Menches [neighbors] with three pictures of the deer Mr. Mench killed. Enclosed was a clipping about Bob Hope landing at Wonsan ahead of us.  We're trying to figure out an answer for it.  We wish to send it along with the clipping to Bob Hope.

The fellows are talking about the Marine Corps at the moment.  A bull session is going on.  When they get tired of talking about the way the Marines operate and why, they'll turn to something else.  One guy likes to tell jokes and stories, but he can never tell it right.  He adds something in that doesn't belong, or he leaves something out.  When we don't get the point, we don't laugh.  He looks at each of us and says, "Oh, oh, something musta went wrong."  After a while he'll start laughing.  He remembered what went wrong.  He tells the story over again and it still doesn't make sense.

Nov. 24, 1950. SuDong. There hasn't been much work, so we spend a lotta time around the stove keeping warm.  The hills around us are covered with snow, but where we are it's damp and cold.

Received a letter with pictures of my family.  Requested a pipe with a bent stem be sent me.  Sent two South Korean bills home.

Nov. 26, 1950. SuDong.  We haven't had any snow except in the hills around us.  We received two big snow plows that can be used on trucks or tractors.  I understand a little farther north they do have snow and ice. The trucks leaving here have chains on all wheels.  The drivers say it's rough.  There is one place they call nine-mile hill.  They say they can't get out of low gear for nine miles.

It's almost 9 P.M.  We had to unload the now plows and some other supplies.  We sent the verse to Bob Hope.  Copy enclosed.  We're afraid it'll backfire on us, although there is nothing in it to hurt anyone.

The wind blew pretty hard yesterday.  Has stopped today and is a little warmer.  Still cold enough to wear a coat and cause us to drop any tools we pick up and try to use without gloves.  Working with gloves isn't easy either.

We got into a big argument about the word jester.  Did we spell it right?  I argued the way it is.  Now it has been sealed, I'm sure it's wrong.  I'm not going to tell these guys, though.  I don't want to look down the barrels of eight rifles.  The altercation got pretty hot.

SuDong, Korea, Nov. 26, 1950
<u>Mr. Bob (Beat us to Wonsan) Hope</u>

Mr. Hope, you landed at Wonsan
and we were left behind;
But from all we can hear there wasn't
a single flying mine.

The town had already been secured,
Not by Army or Navy in their genes,
For you see, Mr. Hope, Republic of Korea
Has their own Marines.

If the planes had brought us in,
And set us down on land,
Then we would have been there
To give you a welcome hand.

We are only fighting men,
It's surely not a jester,
But you'll always find us around
When things begin to fester.

You landed at Wonsan before we did,
That we surely know,
And if we ever have the chance
We're sure to see your show.

To end this little verse
It's not so good you see
But it comes from the Second Squad,
Second Platoon, Auto Maintenance Company.

Composed by
Cpl. Charles Gregary, Little Rock, Ark.
Cpl. Charles J. McManama, Covington, Ken.
Cpl. Fred T. Klemm, Denver, Colo.
Cpl. Doyle H. McMillian, Cleveland, Ohio
Pfc. Victor S. Hando, Wilkes-Barrie, Penn.
Sgt. "GB" Tucker, Amarillo, Texas
Pfc. Harry L. Lay, St. Louis, Missouri
Pfc. Bernie McKeehan, Los Angeles, Calif.
Pfc. William Pardwick, New York, N.Y.

Nov. 29, 1950. Near SuDong. The last couple of nights we just about caught up with the war, or rather it came back on us. It's quiet tonight, in fact, too quiet. We're blacked out, or supposed to be. I'm writing by candlelight. The last couple of nights we've slept with our clothes on and our rifles handy. I keep mine loaded now. There isn't too much to worry about. The infantry is all around us. The only worry is if they break through to us.

The town of SuDong is five or six miles to the south of us. The radio I was supposed to get back in the machine shop was broken beyond repair. The Sgts. have the other one in their tent and I go over and listen sometimes.

We were issued more clothes. Don't know what I'm going to do with them all. Received another suit of longies and I haven't worn any for a couple of weeks. It seems to be a drier cold up here in the hills. Anyway, I don't feel it like I did on the beach. Our clothes are getting pretty dirty. It's hard to wash them because they just freeze. Unless it gets extremely cold, I have no problem keeping warm. It snowed about an inch last night and I felt good all day.

We haven't gotten any mail for a couple of days. Quite often the truck convoys get hit hard.

Some of the fellows are complaining about it being too quiet. I agree, and we have been assigned to guard the equipment compound tonight. The 1st squad is assigned to the tent area. There's a lot of us in the 2nd squad to stand guard. Dividing it equally, we each stand for one hour and 20 minutes. I go on from 0320 to 0440. Three mortars were fired this evening; it has been quiet since.

Dec. 1, 1950. SuDong. It's hard to get a good night's sleep. The Reds keep trying to slip in on us. We're still blacking out at night.

As far as I know, everyone in this unit has all the cold weather gear he needs to keep warm. We've heard stories from the front lines, however, that aren't so good. If only the durn Chinks would stay where they belong.

Dec. 6, 1950. Hamhung. We moved back yesterday and are now a couple of miles outside of Hamhung. We were told we were moving again today. We have done nothing so far today except stand by, look for food, water, and fuel oil for our stoves. We had none of these items. We did have plenty of words to throw around, however. We had a good time beating our gums. It didn't do any good of course. Anyway, we were glad to get out of the hot spot we were in.

Col. Beall is still farther up with the 3rd and 4th platoons. Col. Beall and some of the others rescued 300 Army men from the icy trap they were left in. All were wounded and couldn't do for themselves. [They were survivors of Task Force Faith.][10]

I don't know why we have moved back. The rumors have

it we are to set up a line of defense here. I understand the enemy is within 15 miles of Hamhung. Better than 360 yards like we had it up above. The story has it there are near a million Chinese hammering at our tails. The men up front are having a tough time of it. It was cold and windy last night, but it's a little warmer today. I don't know where we go from here nor why. The whole thing is very confusing. We are having a good time beating our gums. The Regulars are saying we wouldn't be in this mess if it wasn't for the Reserves. We Reserves are saying if we hadn't been so stupid, the Regulars would be in it by themselves. Of course the real reason we are all here is to keep our world the way we want it and so our children can have Xmas in peace and quiet.

Dec. 8, 1950. Hungnam. About half of the 2nd platoon, 1st, and headquarters platoons are set up outside of Hungnam on the road to Hamhung. As we get the story, the 3rd and 4th platoons and the other half of the 2nd platoon are fighting their way out from up north. We expected them tonight, but received word they might not make it until tomorrow night. We put up tents for them and are standing by with hot chow and part of our gear to share with them. Sure glad I wasn't with them. I was up near SuDong until two days ago. We had only one road open to us at the time. It was a bit warm, and I don't mean the weather. We expect to get warm here or even hot. It's only a matter of days or possibly even hours.

It has snowed all day and it's still at it. Not too cold, though. Hope it doesn't get any colder.

From the beginning, this has been a very confusing operation.

We're living in tents with oil heaters.

Some of the men are wondering if it isn't a mistake to tell their wives where they are. She could be holding a letter in her hand dated just a few days before when the radio tells her the town mentioned in the letter is blown apart.

I don't know if we are expected to hold here or not. If we remain, it's almost certain we'll be under fire. I don't see how we can avoid it. The whole thing is very confusing. I never thought I would ever be in this kind of position.

I have guard from 5 to 7 in the morning, one of two men on "listening" post. We're set up in a school yard. Small school-- small kids. They were holding school the day we moved in. Don't think they held any today.

Dec. 15, 1950.  Aboard the Lafayette Victory.  We weren't given a chance to mail letters.  We had only a few minutes to get our gear packed and get on a truck.  We ended up at the dock in Hungnam. Fourteen of us were put on the night shift, and twenty-eight on the day shift.  Some of the men on the day shift were able to write letters and get them mailed by truck drivers.  Most of us weren't able to get letters off.  We arrived at the dock about 5 P.M.  The night shift was put right to work, loading the ship.  We worked straight through until 7 A.M.  No supper, and when we were relieved, I was too tired to eat breakfast.  We all worked hard.  I wasn't the only one to forget breakfast.  We got our gear aboard and went to sleep.  We got chow at 4:30 and went back to work at 6 P.M.  We were relieved at 7 the following morning. The third night we got chow at midnight.  It was a big help.

We're now sitting in the harbor of Pusan in South Korea. I finally caught up on my rest and feel fine.  The chow is very good and there are only 29 of us aboard besides 42 members of the crew.  We're hoping we stay out here awhile.  Once we get into shore, there won't be any more rest.  The ship will have to be unloaded.  They wouldn't feed us aboard ship while we were loading, but we could go up and get coffee whenever we had a slack minute.  To get chow we had to board a truck and go about a mile to an Army mess hall.

The 3rd and 4th platoons got back to our camp before we left. They were trying to find cots to sleep on when we left.  I left mine for them.  They lost all of theirs.  They also lost the two machine shops and most of the trucks they had with them. Everything they had to leave was either burned or blown up.  On the way down, they found some wounded Army men left behind by their units.  They brought them out also.  They also had to destroy a lot of Army equipment still in good condition.  They walked most of the way, carrying the wounded with them.  I doubt very much there will be anything in the papers about Marines finding the wounded Army men and carrying them out.

The rest of the 2nd platoon arrived at the dock the second day after we did.  I don't know why we left North Korea.  I don't know why we're going to Pusan.  It seems we could go on into the dock but are waiting out here because there's a chance the orders will be changed.  They think there's a chance the orders will change to Japan.

This is a private merchant ship with a civilian crew.  The only inspections so far have been made by Sgt. Tucker and those were just to see that our living quarters clean.

Marines weren't properly trained for this action.  Only the veterans of World War II are ready for combat.  Some of the men, or perhaps I should say boys, went into the Reserves and each time they went to summer camp they were increased one rank. We have two Sgts. in our platoon that never went to boot camp and we had to show them how to clean their weapons.  There are several Pfcs. and Cpls. that never went to boot camp and didn't know how to load their weapons, let alone know how to clean them.  These men with us haven't had a hard time of it; but the men in the infantry---and I complained because I didn't get a refresher course.

I notice there's a lot of cameras.  No one has told them at any time they couldn't or shouldn't have them.  During the last war, all cameras were confiscated and burned.  Although there are larger cameras, most are 16 mm, about the size of a cigarette package.

The crew has a washing machine in the head.  It's a domestic type and I'm hoping it stands up under the grind we're giving it.  We should be pretty well cleaned up by the time we go ashore.

The crew is treating us like kings.  "You guys deserve the best.  Any time we can help you out, just say so."  I bet I've heard that at least a hundred times.  And they're making good their word.  Just had lunch:  beef roast, fish for those who wanted it. Now I've got my days of the week straight again.

The guys are pulling tricks on each other, and that's a good sign everything is going to be under control.  One fellow came in here with a pair of handcuffs on.  Someone had slipped them on him in the galley.  He went back with a Russian sub-machine gun (empty), hoping he can scare the guy into giving up the key.

Dec. 17, 1950.  Pusan.  We're unloading the ship.  I'm on the night shift again.  Worked all night.  Rolled out of the sack a little while ago and took a shower.  Unloading the ship is faster than loading it.

Heard the president's speech.  Didn't care for it.  I don't expect to be going home for some time.  [On Dec. 15, President Truman gave a radio and television address on "The National Emergency."  He saw the conflict in Korea as one between free nations, led by the United States, and Communist nations, led by the Soviet Union.][11]

Dec. 20, 1050.  Masan.  We arrived here the day before yesterday.

Sgt. Tucker and I were assigned to ride an LST up from Pusan with three bulldozers, three finger lifts and an ammo carrier trailer. We were the only two from our battalion to ride the LST. Everyone else rode trucks over a road I'm sure I'm glad I missed. Two trucks with trailers were turned over but nobody was hurt. I'm still trying to figure how I got picked to ride the LST. We were moving equipment off the railroad track so the train could get through when I heard my name. I looked around and saw only three officers. I couldn't hear what else they said. However, a little later I saw them talking to Tucker. A little later he told me I was to go with him. I asked how I got picked. He said it wasn't his idea, that they had asked him if he wanted to take me and he had no reason to say no. He didn't want to ride the LST and he thought I didn't also. I'm glad I was on the LST. I was on the list to drive one of the trucks.

We had a lotta fun operating the bulldozers. At first I was scared. No one asked me if I knew how to operate them. I was told to climb aboard a TD 18 and start operating it. When I climbed up on it, I couldn't remember the gear shift, let alone how to start the thing, but as I sat down in the seat it all came back to me. I got it started on gas, let it run a little, then shoved it over to diesel. I noticed the three officers and Tucker watching me. The officers had their hands behind their backs and it occurred to me that those birds had their fingers crossed. It made me mad and cocky. I threw the throttle all the way forward, shoved it in gear, pulled back the lever to lift the blade, then pulled back the clutch lever and backed it out of the place where it was parked, changed gears, pulled on the turning clutch and the 20 tons of metal at full throttle around just close enough to those officers to make them move. I saw them move back and all three folded their arms across their chests and smiled.

I worked with it for awhile pulling trailers off the tracks. Once I had to hook onto a machine shop trailer I hadn't had time to move, and the train ran into it. The train wasn't moving fast and stopped so this machine shop was jammed between the train and another machine shop. I had to pull forward at the same time the train did in order to get the thing out without tearing it apart. I think there was more damage done to the train than the trailer.

When we got down to the LST, I got the grand job of backing the ammo carrier aboard. I got it just inside and the cross bar on the hitch broke. The ammo carrier swung to one side, the pin slipped out, and the ammo carrier slammed into the back of the dozer. Noise? I thought the whole ship was coming apart. The trailer empty weights five tons, to say nothing of the several tons loaded onto it. The ratchet on the tongue that is used to lower a jack when the thing is parked was bent all out of shape. This trailer has tracks on it like a crawler tractor and it is the pride and joy of Col. Beall. He hasn't seen it yet, or at least he hasn't noticed it's bent. I wonder why I don't make Sgt. Anyway, Tucker said it was the first time he had heard me cuss.

Dec. 22, 1950. Masan. Half the company was assigned to work from 12 noon to 12 midnight, the other half from 12 midnight to noon. I'm on the first shift and think it's best. We don't have time for letter writing or even keeping properly clean.

This morning I got up ahead of the other men here in the tent, found some water, and I am trying to heat it to shave and wash. The other men are getting up now.

Received check for $345 yesterday, and I will send it on. It's 10:30 and time is getting short. We eat at 11:30 and go to work at 12. There's plenty of work. The company now has only two machine shops instead of four.

I'd better get going--these guys are using my water.

Dec. 25, 1950. Masan. Merry Xmas. We were allowed the day off and I'm trying to get my clothes washed. We're to get booster-shots at 11 this morning.

Dec. 25, 1950 Masan. We had quite a dinner. I couldn't eat it all. Menu attached.

I got my clothes washed. I did send my field jacket out with one of the native women to wash. I'm afraid to send all my clothes for fear I won't get them back. Some of the other men lost theirs.

The Army's Star-Lighter Band set up outside the shed where we were eating and played for us during the meal. We were also issued three cans of beer--free. We got two cans yesterday. I gave the two away yesterday, but today is Christmas.

We got the day off, except for shots this morning and police call this afternoon. Police call is cleaning up the area. Understand we're to go back to work at 8 A.M.

Dec. 26, 1950. Masan. Saw Bob Wilson this morning. Seemed fine, but homesick. He said the meal yesterday was pretty good, but it was in the wrong location.

Rumor has it we will move back north soon. My work shift is 4 P.M. to midnight. We've been getting our personal gear in order. Time is now 2:30 P.M. We have a lot of trucks and jeeps to overhaul. I hope we get caught up soon. My part of the job is grinding valves, reseating them in the head, changing clutch base plates, clutch liners, recutting brake drums, making bolts and rods, drilling out and removing broken studs, making some parts and sharpening tools, etc.

Dec. 28, 1950. Masan.  We had turkey again today for dinner (lunch). Also real butter.  We can't figure it out.  It was a very nice meal for it to not be a holiday.

Bob Wilson saw me limping around this morning.  I dropped a flywheel on my right foot.  Nothing to worry about; I hurt it just bad enough to make me limp.  I didn't go to sick bay, but may have to yet if it keeps hurting.  I happened last night and I thought by this morning it would be all right, but it's swelled and there's a blue line across the base of my little toe.  When I walk it lets me know it's sore.

Apparently a number of men are to be transferred--possible to the infantry.  Pretty sure I won't be one of them.

The news here is very confusing.  I felt it was a mistake to put MacArthur in charge over here.  I still feel the same way.  I also think the quicker he is removed, the better off we will be.  I just don't think he's the man for the job.

Dec. 29, 1950. Masan.  We had a movie last night.  A-M company was assigned to go at 8:30, the letter companies at 6:30.  I worked in the machine shop until 6:30.  The movie was being shown in the 6X shop.  As I went by, I looked in to see what the movie was and noticed it was a bit empty in back.  A cartoon had just started, it was dark, I thought no one would see me and I would be able to see the movie early and hit the sack early.  Everything went fine until the reel was empty and, of course, to change reels they turned the lights on.  The guy in front of me turned around and Bob Wilson stared me in the face.  Of course he was there, since he's the Special Service Officer.  I quickly says I have some clippings for him and start reaching in my pockets for them.  For the life of me, I couldn't remember which pocket I put them in.  I finally found them in a pocket I had already put my hand in twice.  It never fails.  I do something I'm not supposed to do and I'm sure to get caught.  The name of the movie was "The Admiral was a Lady."

According to the news we get here, the Reds are massing a million men above the 38th for an all-out drive.  This could get interesting yet.

Somebody keeps playing with the lights, and it has started raining.

They changed our shift again.  We went to work at 8 this morning.  Excuse me please--we were supposed to go to work at 8 but none of knew until 8 and the word was given to fall out.  You know what?  There's nine people in this tent and at 8 there are nine people still in the sack, fast asleep.  The MSgt. stuck his head in the tent and in a very nice voice told us what he thought and what he thought, of course, was very nice and educational. Anyway, we fell all over ourselves and each other getting out of the sack and getting our clothes on.  When I got to the machine shop it was five after and I was still buttoning up clothes.  We have more fun.  I think.

Dec. 31, 1950.  Masan.  Understand we are to move again soon. We had one order to move to Pyongyang, but the order was canceled.  Col. Beall was telling us about it at chow formation. We were to have gone by LST.  Now new orders are expected Jan. 3rd or 4th.

Except for rifle inspection, we had today off, and understand we are to have tomorrow off also.  We are to have a movie in the shop.  I could have had liberty yesterday, but didn't figure I had lost anything outside the compound so didn't go.

9:15.  I went and saw the movie:  "The Broken Arrow," an Indian story.  It was based in New Mexico and Arizona.  Very colorful and a good lesson in peace.

Some of the boys are frying bacon on the oil heater.  I think it'll be all right for me to eat some even if they do the work-- seeing as how I was the one who "obtained" the bacon.

I can't quite figure this going back north.  It might be a holding action and then again it might be something else.  There's a good change it'll be a large-scale action.  If so, it'll be on the radio and in the newspapers.  Col. Beall told us for the first time today some of the plans, even if it wasn't much.

Jan. 1, 1951.  Masan.  Twelve noon, New Year's Day, 1951.  Chow is supposed to go at 1430 (2:30).  I understand they're preparing a very nice meal.

Lots of noise last night.  The tank area is on one side of us and the ordnance is on the other.  As far as I know, only one person fired shots in our area, and that was a corpsman.  He walked out in front of the Major's tent and fired a .45 pistol and was promptly locked up.  One man in ordnance was locked up when he was caught lying on top of a rock wall, sniping at the men in the MT area.

I received notice yesterday I had a package at the post office.  Someone told me the post office wouldn't be open today because it was a holiday.  After asking everybody who was supposed to know, but didn't, I "checked out" with the Top Sgt. at eleven o'clock and got my package. I'm now smoking one of two wonderful pipes. The Revelation [tobacco] I received a couple of days ago won't last long now. I have three new pipes now and a pound of Revelation. Wonder where I'll carry the pound can if we move out right away. I'll figure out something. One by one, these guys had pipes sent from home and started smoking them instead of cigarettes. They said I was a bad influence on them. Now, I never said anything at all to them about smoking a pipe. In fact, I've tried to talk them out of it. The more of them who smoke, the less chance I have of getting tobacco.

Jan. 3, 1951. Masan. I understand the Reds are seven miles from Seoul.

It is rumored that it's no longer U.S.M.C., but U.S.M., and we are no longer a part of the Navy. General Cates is a member of the Joint Chiefs of Staff and in now a five-star general. Don't know if all this is true. Haven't heard anything officially. [This plan was not approved by President Truman.][12]

Yesterday the 4th platoon went to Pusan to bring back a slug of trucks. They returned with a slug of ambulance jeeps. Today the same platoon went to the rifle range. The second platoon worked from 8 A.M. to 4 P.M. Oh--yes, almost forgot--we received orders to salute all officers wherever and whenever we meet them. Those don't sound like combat orders to me. I haven't as yet saluted an officer since we left the states. Yes, I did, too--aboard on guard duty. We had a couple of O.D.'s who were rather G.I. Some of the officers go out of the way to catch us making a mistake or slipping in our duties. It tickles me pink when I can catch them in a mistake or making a slip. I've got too much nerve for my own good. I call it to their attention. There's nothing they can do about it as long as I call it to their attention according to regulations. But--it gets me nowhere fast when it comes to recommendation for Sgt.

Well, so much for that. Every so often I hear of someone who had been sent back to the States for discharge. I ask how they did it, but so far nothing I can use.

Jan. 5, 1951. Masan. Col. Beall held a formation yesterday and awarded a Lt. the bronze star, then told us the plans were still going forward to move the division back north. He said the plans changed every day, but the last one worked out was for us to move to Pohang, some 140 miles up the coast. Another plan was for us to move 200 miles up the coast. This move would be made completely by truck while the other move would be made by both LST and truck. On the 200 mile move, three trips would have to be made with the trucks to move the division.

We have the 1st and 7th M.T. Battalions with this division. The 7th doesn't have an auto-maintenance company.

I found out tonight by accident that my specialist or M.O.S. number as it is called now is still 3531 M.T. Driver. I started to blow my top and decided it wouldn't get me any place, so I cooled down and started tracing information. It seems the change was turned down by Headquarters Marine Corps. I'm supposed to get some more answers in the morning. I'm a bit burned up. They give out rates now according to MOS numbers. The top driver rate is Cpl.

Sgt. Pareder left last night for a discharge and home because of four dependents. He had to prove he had them, which took some time. He was in charge of the machine shop I'm working in.

Jan. 6, 1951. Masan. Talked with MSgt. Johnson about my M.O.S. number and it seems there is a lot of trouble about changing it because it's completely out of the M.T. [ motor transport] field. Looks like everybody and his dog has to approve it. He said he had one more officer to see and he was sure he would approve it.

After that, as far as he knew, it would be only a matter of paper work. I asked him if I had made a good enough showing in the machine shop to warrant my requesting the number and he said I certainly had. That made me feel good anyway. He also said I could make Sgt. on the driver number, but couldn't go any farther. I'd thought Cpl. was as far as I could go. Anyway, I don't want to be a truck driver.

Jan. 9, 1951. Masan, Korea. The 2nd platoon has orders to move with the 1st Marine Regiment, supposedly somewhere north of Pohang. The regiment is supposed to take its place in the lines.

Sending $50 money order home.

Jan. 13, 1951. We're camped in a creek bottom some 60 miles north of Masan and what I understand to be about 30 miles south of Pohang. We were supposed to go some 30 miles north of Pohang, but didn't. We're camped on an island in what I would call a river. The stream divides and goes on either side of us, then goes back into the one stream again. In addition to our platoon, there is also the 7th Motor Transport, or one company, that is. Also some other units are up the stream. Understand there are also some Army units up there. Other units are moving up. We're supposed to be with the 1st Marine Regiment, but as far as I can find out, they're on up farther north. Part of the 11th

Regiment is upstream from us.  They have the artillery.  I hope they're the ones firing what we've been hearing all day.

Understand the infantry is running into only North Koreans. I'm tired of trying to figure this business out.  All I know for sure, it's cold here and the wind is blowing.  I don't know what the temperature is, but when the river freezes over, I take for granted it's below the freezing point.

We haven't had too much work to do, but I expect there'll be more when they find us.  They set up two machine gun "listening posts" last night and this platoon caught the guard.  I was lucky because I got the camp "fire watch."  We have the fire watch every night anyway, but I hope we don't get the other again.  I might not be so lucky next time.

We've been working on our tents to keep them from blowing down and we're trying to keep warm.  Some of the men are playing cards--next to the fire, of course.  I have my space next to the fire, too.

Jan. 15, 1951.  Yongchon, Korea.  I'm told the name of the village downstream is Yongchon.  We moved into the edge of Yanchon; had our tents up by noon.  Moved only a few hundred feet--just over the hill--from where we were.  I had thought the village was farther away.  Part of it burned yesterday and last night.  I could see the smoke plainly but didn't know it was a fair-sized town. Don't know how the fire started.

Don't know what's going on.  The South Koreans seem to be on the march.  On our way up from Masan, I'll bet we saw no less than 30,000 of them.  There were at least 10,000 in one group. The word is they're being drafted.  They are apparently being taken right out of the fields and put on the march.  I took a ten-mile ride in a jeep this afternoon and saw thousands more. Some weren't armed, but some had carbines, some Gerand M1s, some '30s, Jap, Russian and Chinese rifles.  A lot of them had the bolt action Russian rifle.  What worries me is, I don't know the difference between friend and foe.

The whole thing is very confusing.  I don't know what's going on, let alone what's supposed to happen next.  As far as I can find out, the U.N. forces are still moving back.  Apparently no attempt is being made to drive them back.  It doesn't make sense to me.

I thought before, and I still feel, it was a mistake to have crossed the 38th parallel, but once it was done, I think we should get enough men, equipment and supplies in here and drive them out once and for all.  I don't think the atom bomb should be used in this Korean conflict at all.  I think it should be used as a last resort only, not because of the destructive force it's supposed to have, but because of the reaction of the people in the other so-called peace-loving countries.

Something I'm wondering about is why the countries who are our allies aren't putting more into this thing. I've seen troops from Canada, Australia, England, Greece, Turkey, and France, but only in small numbers. The British Marine Commandos took quite a beating in North Korea when the U.S. Army retreated and left them in a hole.

The wind has quit blowing and it's easier to take the cold. I helped load some rations for B Company a little while ago and will turn off the generator at 10 P.M. We're using the generator on the machine shop for lights in our tents.

One company of 7th MT is set up with us here. We eat in their mess hall, but we also furnish one mess man and now the guard. We also had to find a burner part for their field range. That's why I made the jeep trip. They wanted one part, I asked the Army for two and got four. I put three extra in the machine shop.

It's 9 P.M. some of the fellows are playing cards, one is reading the <u>Leatherneck</u>, one is cleaning a machine gun, and one is writing a letter: this one.

The thing I like most about this unit is the information they pass out. I guess the reason they don't give out with anything is because they don't know themselves.

I can't get excited about anything any more. I don't volunteer for anything. If the right people tell me something to do, I go and do it. If the wrong people tell me to do something, maybe I do it and maybe I don't. It depends on whether or not it will benefit me by getting it done.

Please send a "Marine Band" harmonica.


Jan. 21, 1951. Andong. It's a bit cold and the wind is blowing. We moved up here yesterday afternoon. The X Corps CP is across the way from us. There are three flags, each on a separate pole, even in height: U.S., U.N., and the Korean Republic.

We couldn't get the engine on the generator started this morning until a few minutes ago. Another ten minutes and we go to chow. I understand the mail is to go out about 1:00. Don't know when we will get any in. None of us are sure of the correct date. I think it's Monday, Jan. 22nd. We were two days getting up here. Hurry up and wait. That's what we did most of the time. Our own officers didn't know what it was all about.

There's lots of rumors around here, but nothing worth repeating. We're supposed to be with the 1st Regiment, but I don't know where they're at. I'm supposing they're a part of the many units around here. We're still with the 7th M.T. too. Their mess hall or galley is set up outside our tent. At least we don't have far to go to eat.

Jan. 23, 1951. Andong. Tuesday. It was rumored the Chinese agreed to a cease fire while they talk about Formosa. Then the rumor the war was over. We're hoping we get official word soon.

We're in a forward area, have two men walking guard together. Our platoon takes care of post #1 while the 7th M.T. Bn. takes care of the other posts including the machine gun "listening" and "outposts." There are 35 of us (Cpls. and below) to walk post. There's 24 on each night in two-hour shifts. Two hours are enough in this cold weather.

Our working hours are 8 to 4:30 with an hour for lunch, seven days a week. We've never had Sunday off--although when church services are announced, any and all men can go for the services, then back to work.

One of the guys came in and said he heard over the radio that the Chinese refused to accept the cease-fire terms.

These guys can't be satisfied to sing songs already written, but they gotta think up their own. Add the train trying to pull up a grade on a by-pass where a bridge was blown out, the Army blasting holes in the frozen earth, and tell me I'm doing a good job writing this letter.

We don't have demolitions. To dig our holes, we pour gasoline on the ground, set it afire to thaw out the dirt, dig a little, more gasoline, more digging, etc. We have nearly all Army gear now, but no demolitions. Some of the other Marine units may have it.

Jan 28, 1951. Andong. I made Sgt. dated Jan. 13th. I wonder how I did it. I feel I'm accomplishing a little bit, anyway, considering the company was already over-rated with 30 Sgts. and 60-some Cpls. Three of us in the platoon made Sgt. and three Cpl. I'm the only Reserve. All the others are Regular and were with the brigade.

It seems there's some type of bill before Congress, or perhaps it's passed by this time, on insurance. Apparently, we get $10,000 free insurance. Can't find out anything about it here.

Jan. 31, 1951. Andong. Understand my pay goes up $13 per month including overseas pay. I don't walk guard post any more and don't have to take certain things off certain guys. Of course they don't shove it at me any more. This platoon now has nine Sgts., three SSgts., one MSgt. and two Warrant Officers. We three new Sgts. were told to move into the Sgts.' tent. We said we were satisfied. So far they haven't forced us to move. We're taking quite a beating from the fellows. There are two of us in this tent. No matter what we do, there's wise cracks made. We don't pay attention, but I'm beginning to understand why they separate the ranks.

We were trying to figure out last night what to do with the Christmas cards they passed out to us. One man said he was going to write on his: "Up your leg and down your spine, won't you be my Valentine?" Also, "Down your spine and up your leg, won't you be my Easter egg?" I sent ten cards.

Rumor has it we're again headed for the States soon. Hope it's true. Do we ride again over the road the devil built or do we go to the States?

The 2nd platoon is the only one not with the company now in Pohang, an east coast seaport. The work has been light the last two days. We're cleaning up the machine shop inside and out, greasing the wheel bearings, tuning up the engine and cleaning the generator, etc. The welders are doing the same thing to their equipment. The mechanics haven't had much to do except take care of their tools and play cards. Much of the time during the last two weeks, we two machinists have been the only ones working.

We heard about a bonus to be paid for combat service about a week ago. If it goes through, the money will come in handy.

The weather here has been nice the last few days. It's warm enough to work in our shirt sleeves. We even jumped into a truck yesterday and went down to the water point where we took showers. The heated showers in tents have been set up about a week. Yesterday was the first time we were permitted to go. It sure felt good.

Accidental discharge in the next tent. Some people never learn. Seems nobody hurt.


Feb. 4, 1951. Andong. We had a rifle inspection yesterday. "Mr." Winn, one of the warrant officers with our platoon, inspected. When he got to me he asked, "You just made Sgt., didn't you, Klemm?" I said, "Yes, Sir." He wanted to know who else made Sgt. I told him, "McManama and Eilings." He didn't check my rifle very close. I knew something was up. When the inspection was over, the three of us were told to fall out and take over and give the platoon close order drill. Oh, brother.

I had never before given commands in close order drill. Still haven't. Eilings was first. Nobody had done any close order drill since they left the States. Several who had never been through boot camp had never been through any of it. It turned out quite a mess. The three of us were told to stand by and watch. So we stood by, watched, got cold, and laughed while the three staff Sgts. put the rest of the platoon through the works. All three of the Staff went at it at the same time. One gave the commands while the other two worked in and around the platoon. When the command, "Right shoulder arms," was given, a half dozen men put the rifle on their left shoulders. "Your other right, stupid," was the next command. We're supposed to do an hour of close order drill every day, but we didn't today.

The morning following the evening I was told I had made Sgt., all nine of us Sgts. had to make out what they call "Fitness Reports." It seems they have to be made out every six months. The report includes my duties, names, ages of my children, etc. Most of the space is left for the officer in charge to fill out. It seems I'm to be graded on everything I'm involved in as to whether I did the job poorly, good, excellent, etc.

I was told if I had seven years in the Corps I could draw an extra $67.50 per month for family allowance. I could only count up to five. Reserve time counts.

Mr. Mickells, the warrant officer in charge of this platoon, went to Pohang yesterday to find out what's expected of us and I think he was going to find out if my M.O.S. number had been changed. If not, he was going to put in a formal request to have it changed. He says if it hasn't been changed yet it has to be signed by the commandant in Washington now that I'm a Sgt. Cpls. and below can be changed by the Division Commander on recommendation of the unit commanders. Since the number I want is outside the Motor Transport functional field, there are several officers who have to sign. Sounds like a lot of red tape. They tell me it works both ways, though. The unit commanders can't change the number either just to fulfill their own desires. I don't recall they paid as much attention to these numbers during the last war. They still don't have to assign jobs according to the number though. If they did, I wouldn't be in the machine shop.

Sgt. Michich, the other man in the machine shop, has a maintenance supply number. We asked about getting his changed to machinist too. He was told it would be impossible because he had made both his Cpl.'s and Sgt.'s rates on the one he has.

Michich is 21, single, full of vim, vinegar, and vigor and such. In other words, he runs circles around me. He did not go through boot camp, and he has not been in the service before. He's a good worker and knows machine shop work. He can remember what size drill it takes for a certain size tap. I can't.

For the last four days, a young punk has spent a lot of time around the machine shop, asking us to do this and do that. We were beginning to get provoked with him when yesterday afternoon he showed up with his bars on. Not only is he an officer, but he spent the last four years before coming over here as a machine shop instructor in the engineers at Camp Lejeune. I showed my surprise, of course. He said he kept coming back to us because we were the only ones he had found over here who could do a decent job. At present, he's an officer in the engineers. Can you tie that? I didn't tell him I never went to machinist school. We both stood and looked at him like a couple of nuts until he laughed and left.

Feb. 6, 1951. Andong. I gave the commands at close order drill yesterday and surprised myself. When I first took over the platoon, I had a bit of stage fright, but it left me as soon as I gave the first command. Now the guys can't believe it was my first time. They say I did it like an expert.

Rumor has it that all members of the brigade will assemble at Pohang the 14th to leave Korea.

We've had some arguments here about close order drill. Now it's almost time for lights out. It's my job to shut off the generator every night.

I don't know what's up. Everything's quiet. When we have time to do close order drill, you can be sure there isn't much doing. What burns me up is that when we get a little time and think about washing clothes or writing letters, some bright boy thinks up stuff like close order drill. The argument has started again. Just try to think of something straight to write. Someone found a book some place. Some gung-ho dope brought one with him; one of the staff, I think.

Might as well go listen to five minutes of the news and after that turn off the lights.

Feb. 8, 1951. Andong. No need to worry about me here at Andong. There are a few stray Reds around. They call them guerrillas. We pick up a few every now and then, but there's nothing to worry about.

It's snowing now, but doesn't feel too cold.

There's talk about us moving again in a few days. Don't know where. The Gooks (natives) say we're going to Seoul. I can't see it. Anyway, Seoul is still in Red hands. But then, on the other hand, these Gooks seem to know more about what we're doing than we do. I might say they've been right before. They've told us on other occasions where we were going before even the officers received word and they were right.

This company has several Korean natives with it. None of us could pronounce their names or remember them, so we nicknamed them. The one we have with our platoon is Taillite; others are Sparkplug, Flywheel, Flat-tire, Valvestem, etc.

I came into the tent yesterday and a strange native was sitting on one of the sacks (cots) playing a harmonica. He was playing American pieces in a way that would put me to shame. We started making signs at him in an effort to question him. He, in very good English, told us he could not only speak it, but he was an English teacher in Seoul High School and some day soon he would again be teacher of English in high school in Seoul. He turned out to be very interesting. The guys told him I was a teacher back in the States and I couldn't get him to understand otherwise.

He said, "I do not understand. English soldier speak English. American soldier also speak English, but no sound same." Of course the guys put in to make it clear to him we were Marines, not soldiers. He said, "I know, I know, Marines No. 1, Army No. 2." Then he went on to say, "American soldier say many words I not understand. I try to teach to students, but no can find in dictionary. Me no understand." We tried to explain they were slang and cuss words and not to be taught in school. He never understood.

He had a pistol he was pretty proud of. He said he had gotten it from an American soldier who lost on the deal. "American soldier did not want to part with it, but finally gave in for $20 American money. Only one like it in Korea. I tooken American soldier." We took one look at his pistol. It was in all probability the only one like it in Korea alright, but it was him got took. It was an air pistol that shoots .22 cal. pellets. "No can find ammo," he told us. When we told him what it was he said, "Only pistol like it in Korea, very rare, me find Korean soldier with .45 colt, me trade. No other like it in Korea, very rare."

I would like to be with this guy for a few weeks. He said a person who puts his mind to it can learn the Korean language in one week. He said the Korean language is easy because each character means only one thing, while with English one character could mean several different things. For example, the letter C is used for the letter K, etc.

Feb. 11, 1951. Andong. The fifth day without mail.

It's been snowing. It snowed and rained all night and all day. The result is mud---. I'm glad I'm working in the machine shop.  The mechanics get wet when they work on the top side of a truck or jeep, but it's worse when they have to crawl underneath and lie down in the mud.  It makes it even worse when the wind blows and it gets cold.

Close order drill was knocked off the last few days, but I understand we're to have it again in the morning.  Also typhus shots at 9:30.


Feb. 13, 1951.  Andong.  Mail today.  There's a rumor now that we will be rejoining the company in Pohang soon.  I hope not. We operate pretty good as a platoon.

We received another truck load of parts this morning. One of the drivers told me they were treating men pretty dirty down there.  What he meant was they are being very G.I. and I don't like that.  He said he and the other drivers had to go out yesterday and move their trucks because they were parked on the parade ground and they were going to have a parade.  He said he saw part of the parade and when they left, medals were being awarded.  He didn't know who were getting the medals or what for.  No one there is allowed to wear the fur caps and no greens which are warmer than dungarees.  It seems at one time half the company was in the brig. Apparently it's very easy to get thrown into the brig in Pohang. According to the stories I've heard, a lot of men have been demoted and fined heavily in addition to spending some time in the brig.  According to what I've been told, some of the men have been arrested for good reason, while others were arrested for almost nothing.  All you have to do is get some officer or staff or Sgt. mad at you and he will lay for you, watch for some infraction they can hold you on and your goose is cooked.

We're going to miss the train coming up the grade when we leave here.  We can hear it coming from way off, making a run for this steep grade. It's become a habit with us to make motions along with the piston strokes.  Sometimes it makes it and sometimes it doesn't.  More often it doesn't.  It's just like the little story we used to read in the first primer.  "I think I can--I think I can--I think I can--I think I can--I thought I could--I thought I could."  Then a whistle to waken the dead, letting everyone know he made it.  It happens during the night and we wake up and listen.  "Will he make it this time?"  The suspense almost gets us down until he either makes it or the driver slips and he has to back up and try again.  Usually there's two or three engines. When three engines can't make it, it must be a heavy load.

We've been hearing about the cold weather back in the States.  Sometimes we hear news on the radio and sometimes we get the <u>Stars and Stripes</u>.

Feb. 18, 1951. Chungju. We got moved up here last night. We aren't far from Onju. Don't know just how far, but believe it to be about 12 miles. We're supposed to be here about six days. On the way up, the rear axle on the machine shop broke. More fun.

It's been snowing off and on all day. The ground is wet and causes us a little trouble.

I saw one of the officers from Denver. He told me over half of the men who left Denver with our unit have been killed, wounded or frost-bitten.

Almost time for lights out. Heard on the radio it has been left to MacArthur whether or not we cross the 38th again. I guessed we were moving to Wonju, and I didn't miss it by much.

Feb. 19, 1951. Chungju. No mail since we arrived here. I hear they're sending men home under some type of system, but haven't been able to find out much about it. One thing for sure: they aren't sending very many back.

They're putting up a shower on the bank of the river just below us. I hope they let us take a shower once in a while. I'm getting to need one pretty bad.

This is Saturday night and of course there's lots of cowboy and hillbilly music, such as the "Grand 'Ole Opry." Almost everybody flocks around the radio. There's two radios. One the Sgts. have in their tent and one in the 4th squad tent. I can go to either one, of course, and will go to the Sgts. tent when I finish this letter. The guys in the 4th squad make too much noise. I understand the officers found a radio some place today. We've been looking for one for our tent, but without success.

Feb. 21, 1951. Chungju. Three days ago, Col. Beall came up and brought a lot of work with him. I'm trying to figure out how one person could bring so much work with him.

The rest of the company is supposed to move up here today. I don't know if they're going to camp here or go to Wonju. Anyway, I expect we'll be moving soon again. I hope the company brings our mail with them. It started raining this morning and is still raining this evening. I hope it stops before we have to move. Some of the fellows are fueling trucks that came up in the convoy.

According to what I was told, we Sgts. were supposed to make out fitness reports every six months. They handed me another one to sign the other day. It wasn't filled out and I was only to sign my name. It was the same with all the others. I signed it as all the others did.

I hear lots of rumors of men going back to the States. First it's a point system, then they are drawing lots, some are getting out because of dependents, etc. Also there's the story that regardless of the system, specialists are frozen, meaning machinists, of course. When I heard that one, I said my M.O.S. was truck driver. I got told off. The letter is in to have the number changed and I was no longer to refer to myself as a truck driver. I'm a machinist. That makes me laugh. I can't help think of the training I've had in machine shop practice. As far as I can recall, I've received a little training in everything but machine shop work. I wonder what kind of work I'll be doing next. Jack of all trades, master of none.

Feb. 28, 1951. Wonju. Got moved here yesterday. The battalion is supposed to be up here in three or four days and we've received word there's to be no food in the tents, no cooking or heating food on the heaters. We're a lot happier when we're away from the battalion. We've lots more freedom.

March 2, 1951. Wonju. We all had to work last night and get some trucks ready to go on a convoy to Inchon.

I understand some more men are being sent back to the States. All were members of the brigade. All are Regulars and will be re-assigned to posts in the States or some other permanent station. I'm told 20 more are to go soon from this unit. Apparently they'll also be from the brigade. Perhaps when they get around to the Reserves, I'll have a chance to come home. Rumor has it that no discharges will be given to anyone, except maybe a few, who will be declared "not available." Everyone else will be assigned to inactive duty. Some of the other platoons are arriving and some of the men are crowding in here to get warm. It turned quite cold yesterday. The wind's blowing and it's hard to do any work.

We pulled our machine shop up here behind the wrecker. Two of us rode the back of the wrecker which wasn't bad at all. We thought a few times we would lose the machine shop. I believe at least half the time it was riding on only two wheels.

When the other started over the pass with their machine shops and parts trailers, they got cold feet and now are holding them some place down below until they can get a train running, which may be a week or more.

March 1, 1951. Wonju. It's 8 P.M. and I just got secured from work. I have to go back to sick bay at 9 again and let the Doc check my eye again.  He's worried I'll get infection in it.  I got a piece of steel in it from the emery wheel.  Nothing to worry about. It's just a bit worrisome trying to write, work or even get around with just one eye.  The other has a patch over it.  The Doc got the piece of steel out, but he says it cut through the protective tissue covering the cornea and he said a lot of big words about it. Anyway, he doesn't want infection to set in.  Neither do I.

Received harmonica yesterday.  It's just what I wanted.
"Ole One Eye."


March 6, 1951.  Wonju.  Yesterday and today they've had me on no duty.  The first day, the Doc didn't understand the type of work I was doing.  When I told him the second time I was working in the machine shop, it struck home and he blew his top. I'm now on no duty, "and absolutely no reading."  The eye is coming along real well.  There's nothing to worry about.  The Doc is more worried about it than I am.  He was even going to send me to the hospital in Japan by air.  He's afraid of infection.

I failed to mention one thing I can do:  play the harmonica. When I first pulled it out of the package, they all groaned.  When I started to play it, they all looked and then got silent.  A little later, they started singing with me.

It snowed heavy here last night and almost all day.  It isn't very cold however, and the snow is melting.

We're working the daylight hours.  I say we; I will be, when the Doc takes me off of no duty.  There's a lot of trucks to work on.  There's a 60 some-odd on the dead line, which means we're that much behind.

They're putting a new engine on the machine shop to turn the generator.  It sure looks nice.

Don't worry about me--I'm just "ole one eye."


March 8, 1951.  Wonju.  Just saw a movie, "The Halls of Montezuma."  Purely a war picture and purely for civilians.  We picked it to pieces.  Some of the scenes were real and were put into the film in the right places. The rest of the picture was made at Camp Pendleton.  Some of the scenes I actually saw and took part in myself.

I saw the movie and feel fine.  In other words, my eyes are all right.  The Doc let me go back to work yesterday.  I borrowed some dark glasses and got along just fine.

We're supposed to move up about 12 miles in a few days. We're giving every support possible a motor transport unit can give.  We're getting trucks and jeeps in to overhaul which are beyond repair.  Land mines and booby traps have and still are taking their toll.  This is known as "Operation Killer."  The order is, "Kill everything that moves."

So much for that.  I'm still assigned to the machine shop.

Mail is slow coming because only ammo, food and supplies are being brought up.


March 9, 1951.  Wonju.  Understand we're to move soon to Hoengsong.  That's a little town 12 or 13 miles north of here.

My M.O.S. was turned down again.  Now I'm told I can't get it changed now I'm a Sgt, and Sgt. is as far as I can go with my present M.O.S.  It was suggested I could take a bust, get demoted in other words, go through machinist school, then get my number changed.  Nuts.  I don't expect to make the Corps my life's work anyway.  So much for that.


March 13, 1951.  Hoengsong.  The entire battalion has gotten moved up here and just in time to receive the announcement we are to move again soon.  Don't know how far or where.

Our lights are now tied into the big generator so I don't have to worry about staying up and turning off the generator at 10.

Heard about the Marines hitting the States.  Hope my turn comes soon.  I'm not counting on it until I get there.

I said before and I say again, there's no reason for worry.  I'm just as safe here as I would be crossing the street in Denver.  I hope you realize what this rotation plan is.  I haven't heard anyone say anything about discharges.  The only reason I want to get back to the States is I think I'd have a better chance to get out.  If I have to stay on active duty, I'd just as soon be over here.  There's less foolishness thrown at us by the command.  I'd like for it to happen the same way as last time:  discharge within a few days after I hit the States.  Only I know it won't.  The most I can hope for is assignment to inactive duty.  Might as well get used to it:  it could happen again.

It seems to make Sgt. someone had to sponsor me.  I learn something new all the time, except the name of the person who sponsored me.  Something else, too--I don't get the warrant until six months after it's dated.  I'm on probation for six months.

I learn something new almost every day.  Some of it doesn't make me feel too good.  Even if they should give me a discharge, which I don't think they will, I'll still be subject to a law reading "Ten years or until the man is 45."  We've been told, and I saw it in print, the law has never been put into effect--but I know some men who are over here now that didn't belong to any reserves.  They are wondering how they got over here if the law wasn't put into effect.  They just received telegrams ordering them to report to duty within 24 hours.  Needless to say, they're pretty bitter.

Several men in the company have radios now.  One just gave the time, 9:55.  Newscast now on.  One man received a small radio in the mail today, and I think it was the one I just heard.  We haven't been able to hear a radio in our tent before.

The lights are left on until 11 now because we work the daylight hours.  I'm the guy who said I could go to bed early now.

March 15, 1951.  Hoengsong.  Last night the fellows in the tent got together and bought a radio.  At least we dare to call it that.  We haven't been able to get much on it yet.  Some of the boys are trying to tune up.  It cost me $4 and four of six cans of beer I got last night.  It was the first beer we've been able to get for some time, six cans for 70¢.  The total cost of the radio was $10 and 21 cans of beer.  We got it from the fellows in another tent who got a new radio through the mail.

Col. Beall is on his way back to the States.  He gave us a speech this morning.  Maj. Beroro made Lt. Col.  He was Executive Officer of the battalion, and he will now be in command. Major Roberts, who was commander of A-M company is now battalion executive.  Capt. Sailers will be commanding the A-M Co. He hasn't been around very long, but most of the Regulars seem to know him and say he's all right.  Lt. Raper is company ex, or asst. commander.

All but two of us in the tent went to a movie we heard was showing a short distance from here.  Maybe I'll end up playing with the radio.

"Duffie's Tavern' is on now.  Five minutes of news is just over.  They announced 1500 Marines would land at San Francisco.  Some of the fellows from other tents without radios are in here now.  The news also says 1500 Marines, along with Gen. Smith and Gen. Puller, the two top men of the 1st Marine Div., are to be relieved by May 1st.  Maybe my turn will come--as I'm sure it will, sooner or later.

March 17, 1951.  Hoengsong.  I haven't told you about Jim.  He is a little Korean boy we picked up in Andong and made our house boy.  He's not very big, but he did a pretty good job of keeping our tent clean and seeing to it our water cans were kept filled.  We brought him along with us, but now the order is no house boys-- get rid of them.  So tomorrow morning we're going to put him aboard a truck in a convoy and send him back to Andong.

March 20, 1951. Hongchon. Moved today about 25 miles north of Hoengsong. Tents are set up and everything's under control. The second platoon is all moved up. I understand the entire battalion will be moved in three or four days. We're not very far from the 38th parallel now. I had guessed before that we might end up in Seoul again, but now I'm not so sure.

We have the generator on the machine shop running for our lights again so I have to shut it off at 10.

March 21, 1951. Hongchon. Some more of the company and part of Auto-supply came up today. Also battalion headquarters.

The ground here is pretty soft. A detail has been shoveling sand all day for it to be trucked in. It's going to take a lot of sand to cover the entire area. They way they're setting up, it would seem they're planning on staying here for awhile.

We're all wondering when some more men will be sent back to the States. We were given to understand the Marines arriving in the states did a lot of talking about the other branches of the service. (Army, of course.) They were in the limelight and reporters asked a lot of questions. Anyway, we were told if we couldn't say anything good about the other branches of the service, to keep our mouths shut. I don't know what the Marines are supposed to have said, but I've a good idea.

I'll be glad when my turn comes to go home. I'm not having it bad. Actually, I'm having it very lucky. However, I'm getting tired of it.

March 23, 1951. Hongchon. I sent home a check for $85. My pay is supposed to be $142 plus allotment of $85. Reserve time counts, and I have a total of five years. The pay supposedly is raised every two years. The $142 includes overseas pay, according to the best I can find out. If I had seven or more years in, I would also receive $67.50 per month for family allowance. So much for that.

Some more men are getting ready to go back to the States. According to rumors, all are to be rotated by June 1st. It looks as though I'll be one of the last to leave. That's all right. I'd rather stay a little longer and then go back to the States and stay there, than leave early and come back again.

March 24, 1951. Hongchon. Tomorrow is Easter.

We've been flooded with brake drums to turn and brake shoes to line. We turned out three truck heads today, too. That is, we ground the valves and valve seats and tapped them in. Just in one machine shop with two Sgts. doing the work. Oh, yeah, we also ran some threads on some bolts.

Some of the guys had a big ball game after work. The platoons played against each other. It seems the 4th platoon won.

There's only two in the tent now besides myself. The rest have gone to a movie. I don't know what's playing and anyway, I'm too tired to go. Sgt. McManama is trying to get the radio to work. We can hear the barn dance on in another tent, and are disgusted with our radio. One of these days we just might toss the thing out.

Understand the inactive Reserves are to be sent home and discharged. They are getting names straight today. I said I wanted to be one and they laughed at me. Said specialists like me were wanted and I pointed out my M.O.S. number hadn't been changed. They stopped laughing, but so what? They're short quite a number of motor transport men and they aren't getting enough replacements.

We had a rifle inspection this morning. Our rifles were all right, but some of us got called for wearing dirty clothes. I had clean ones, but failed to change into them. They don't give us much time for washing clothes. We work seven days a week. Working hours now are 7:30 to 5:30 with an hour for lunch.

We were told today _if_ anyone wanted to go to church tomorrow, they could get off long enough to go, but to be sure and get right back to work.

March 28, 1951. Hongchon. It's raining here this evening. Mud and more mud. I'm glad I'm working in the machine shop.

I had my toughest job assigned to me today, to turn a tapered hole in a pulley, which has to fit a tapered shaft on a compressor. We don't have the proper tools, so I'm turning it out with a boring bar on the lathe. We don't have any tapered reamers. We get lots of jobs we don't have tools for, and have to improvise. Sometimes we make tools so we can go ahead with the job. This is the toughest job ever handed me. It must be remembered, too, I've never had any machine shop training.

There are always a lot of people around to tell me what or how, but somehow it never works. I have to figure it out on my own. Their suggestions sometimes give me ideas, such as picking up a hammer and beating in some heads.

Some of the men are getting ready to leave April 1st. All in this company were members of the brigade.

It's 9:30. I never seem to have the time to do what I want to do. I still have to shave.

The company clerk came to the machine shop this

morning with a typed sheet. It read something like, "ask Sgt. Fred Klemm the date he was put on extended active duty and if he had had any deck courts (a type of disciplinary action) since that date." It was signed by someone at Division HQ. The clerk didn't know what it was for and a couple of Staffs that sleep in the same tent with the Top Sgt. said they just want to get the record straightened out. Their records must be in quite a mess if they don't know when I was called to active duty and whether or not I've had a deck court.

April 2, 1951. Hongchon. We worked late last night. I got to hit the sack at midnight. Some of the others worked a little later. I worked again this evening for about an hour after supper to finish a brake drum I was turning down.

One of the Sgts. is going home tomorrow. "Proved" he had four dependents. As soon as he gets moved out, I'm to move into the Sgts.' tent. The other two Sgts. that aren't living in the Sgts.' tent are due to leave on rotation plan the 5th and 6th.

I guess we're to move again in a few days. Anyway, we're supposed to get all the trucks repaired we can.

We sold our radio for $20.

April 5, 1951. Hongchon. Understand the battalion is moving in the next few days. The 2nd platoon is to remain behind. The 3rd is in Hoengsong.

It'll be nice to receive a dividend check. If they also pass the bill to pay all of us in Korea an extra $50 per month, it'll add to our savings.

As I understand it, all the men that have been sent back to the States under the rotation system are Regulars. I understood before they were to be assigned to stations in the States as instructors, etc. I have been feeling around. The best I can learn, I will have a choice of available stations.

The news is on now. There's a radio in here. Oh, I moved into the Sgts. tent. Nothing but buck Sgts. in here. Anyway, put the news along with orders we've been given, it "ain't" good.

There's still nothing to worry about as far as I'm concerned. I'm still one of the lucky ones, even if I am working myself silly. What I mean by that is, we're putting out more work now than we ever have before. Brakes and brake drums are coming in heavy. We can't keep up with it.

We were ordered to turn in all cold weather gear. All we have left now is our sleeping bags.

The 2nd platoon worked last night. The 4th has it tonight, but they don't have a machine shop. No need to tell you what's happening.  We just chased a guy out who wanted the threads traced in a big nut.  I feel sorry for the guys, trying to do work with nothing to do it with.  We've already gone out four times to do little jobs for them.  It could get to be a habit.  And here I wanted to get to bed early.  Oh, well.

April 6, 1951.  Hongchon.  Just got in from work at 8:30 P.M.  Put some clothes on the stove to heat up so I can wash time.  I also need to wash and shave.

A guy just came to get some washers and I'm trying very hard not to have to go out, but I might as well go and get rid of him.  He sure isn't going to go by himself...Well, he got the washers.

Was told today the 3rd platoon was to get a new machine shop to replace the one they lost up north.  Either Sam Michich or I will be transferred to the 3rd platoon and put in charge of it.  I expect it to be me since Sam is already in charge of this one.  The men that operated the old one are now mechanics, not by their own choice, but because of their own fault, as I understand it.  One or both of the men in the 1st platoon shop are about to lose their positions also.  Sam and I have been told by several officers we do more and the best work of all the machine shops in the division.  There's lots of them too--such as the engineers, ordnance, combat service, etc.

Sgt. Stewart, the man I replaced in the Sgts.' tent when he left for home, is the same man who was driving a truck shortly after we landed at Inchon and got stuck.  Some 30-odd Reds jumped him and he had to shoot his way out.  He killed 12 of them and then spent two weeks with the ROKs.

April 9, 195.  Hongchon.  I notice they don't identify the Marines anymore on the newscasts here, or from the Armed Forces radio in Japan.  There's also a U.N. station.  Both mention the activity of the U.S. Army, but when it comes to the Marines, they are referred to as U.S. police forces or U.S. forces.  Maybe the Marines have been heard about too much.  Oh, well---.

We're overloaded with work now.  For several weeks I've been earning my pay and making up for time when I did almost or less than nothing.  The last few days Sam and I have done nothing but eat, breathe and dream in our sleep of brake drums and brakes. We've been swamped and still are.

At 10 o'clock this morning, some guy I had never seen before came up to me and said he had six trucks that he wanted all the brake drums and brakes worked over.  Would I please have them done by noon.  They hadn't been removed from the trucks which isn't our job anyway. There were and still are more than a dozen trucks on the dead line waiting for Sam and me. That isn't all: our motor wouldn't start this morning. Without it, we don't have electric current. No current, no work. In other words, our equipment won't operate. I was working with the motor at the time this guy came up and spoke to me. Everybody's in a hurry; everybody wants us to do their jobs in less than no time at all. Without looking around, I told the guy where he could go. I guess he went there...because I haven't seen him since. One of the fellows standing close by said, "That was an officer, Pappy."

April 10, 1951. Hongchon. The 2nd platoon is all that's left here now. The work has slacked off some. The company moved to Chunchon.

Listening to the news. Not much of interest. Somebody wants MacArthur to report in person to Congress. I'm willing to bet he doesn't. (Note added later: I would have lost.)

April 11, 1951. Hongchon. Heard on the radio Gen. MacArthur has been relieved of his command. No comment---.

Spent the entire day turning brake drums. This morning I had the lathe, the drum lathe that is, sitting on the ground beside the machine shop. After lunch, Sam and I moved it inside the parts tent nearby and ran a cord from the shop for current. I'd just gotten started with the first drum when it rained. A little while later, it hailed. I had started my eighth drum since noon when I was secured at 5 o'clock. There's still six more waiting to be turned. Before those six are turned, others will be brought in. Sam is relining the brake shoes. Of course, we still have to take care of the other work at the same time. There isn't so much of it at present, and we're glad.

April 13, 1951. Hongchon. Friday. It's very nice here: sun shining and very warm. I even went down to the river and took a shower. Our work has slacked to the extent I got the afternoon off. Boy, did I sleep.

April 16, 1951. Chunchon. Moved here yesterday. We're again with the company and the battalion.

The lights keep going out. We like our own little generator the best, but we aren't allowed to use it when we're with the company. They just got a new big diesel job and I think it's the dopes they have working with it.

There's some indication I'll be back in the States before the summer is over. More of the officers are making statements that all the Inchon men are to be out of here not later than June 1st.  However, we heard on the radio that the Marines were to slow down their rotation system.  Unless it gets too rough on the front lines, I have a feeling I will be homeward bound.  I believe I'll be one of the last ones on the list for the rotation system.  I'm expecting them to take the men from the line companies first which is all right with me.  Understand some of the Inchon men have already left from the line companies.

10 o'clock, lights out.  On flashlight.  I'm being told to put out the light--including my pipe--nuts to 'em.

April 20, 1951.  Chunchon.  Oh-oh and oh-brother!  I feel silly.  Everything's under control, but---

We were all teasing Sam, telling him he wasn't going home, he was going to stay in Korea.  Five minutes later, an officer walks in and sits down on the sack beside Sam.  "Two Inchon men from this platoon are going home.  We have two machinists.  Tomorrow morning the platoon will draw numbers to see who goes first.  Klemm is a vet of the last war, he also has a family, so rather than take the chance on both of you drawing numbers 1 and 2 you won't draw."  Not a word for word and <u>not the way we understood it at first, but the way it ended up.</u>  We were talking about it later, and we all agree what he said first was I was going home and Sam would have to wait awhile.  Well, that was all right and we started teasing Sam again while the officer was still here.  Then one of the Sgts. asked if the platoon wasn't going to draw and he said, "Yes."  Then the words I have already put down came out.  What we want to know now is how he knows I am going to draw number 1 or 2, and not maybe the last number.  There's 31 Inchon men to draw.  As I see it, I have as good a chance to draw #31 as I have #1.  If I do, they still aren't gaining anything.  A few minutes ago, we could hear the officer in the staff tent having a fight with Lisenberry.  The staff doesn't get to draw either.  But that wasn't what the fight was about.  Lisenberry thinks Sam should draw too.  I kept trying to think of something to break the thing while the officer was here, but with the guys teasing Sam I couldn't think.  When they realized what had really happened, they shut up, but it was too late.  Sam has already hit the sack and isn't saying one word.  Very unusual.  He's always the last.  It was several minutes after the officer left he realized he wasn't drawing.

Everyone thinks I should go home first, including Sam, but the way it's being done just doesn't set right.  Now, you know why I feel silly.

A battalion formation was held yesterday, and several

men received awards, including Lisenberry.

April 21st.  Drew No. 1.  Leave about the 1st.

April 21, 1951.  Chunchon.  Everything's under control.  I'll be on my way back to the States soon.  I understand at this time, I'll go by truck to Hoengsong, by plane to Pusan, by ship to Kobe, Japan, by ship to the States.  This doesn't mean I'll get out of the Marines.

I was called into the Top's tent where I was told the Col. had approved my going.  The Top wanted my address while on leave.  He told me I had one of two choices, guard duty or FMF (Fleet Marine Force).  There are FMF stations all over, including the States.  I told him I wanted a discharge.  He said, "Can't help you."  I then asked about assignment to inactive duty.  "Can't help you.  If you choose guard duty, you're sure to get stuck in some desert somewhere guarding some ammo dump.  And when they need somebody to go overseas again, those are the guys they take first.  Anyway, you can work on a discharge when you get back to the States.  I can't help you here."  I chose FMF.  I'm supposed to get a 30-day leave shortly after arriving and then report to my new station.  It could be any one of several places in the United States.

I asked about getting my M.O.S. changed.  Absolutely not. Found out something else, too.  No Reserve has gone above Sgt. over here.  Also, there's no directive for anyone to go above Sgt.

I think Sam will come out all right.  Of course he's still lower than the bug that crawled under the carpet.  Everybody raised such a howl they, or rather Lisenberry, let him draw.  He got #6.  The Top says it'll stand.

After what happened last night, you can well understand how I felt when I reached in and pulled out the little rolled up piece of paper.  I was the 11th to draw.  None of us yet knew Sam would get to draw.  I unrolled the piece of paper.  I looked at the 1. The others had yelled out their numbers so a SSgt. could record it.  I couldn't yell the number I had drawn.  Everybody was watching me.  Right in front stood Sam, looking at me, his hands in his pockets, a big smile on his face, tears in his eyes.

I handed the piece of paper to the SSgt. and walked away. A little while later everyone was shaking my hand and telling me how glad they were and all that kind of stuff.  No one holds it against me even if a few wise cracks were made.  The drawing was fair and square.  Of course everyone in the company knew of the set-up with Sam.

I'll tell the Top any packages arriving will belong to the 2nd platoon. These next ten days are going to go awful slow.

There's 15 Inchon men going home from this company. They've told us what we can take with us. I've got a lot of junk to get rid of and I can't very well turn it in. I can give part of it to the new replacements. But there's some nobody wants because they already have it and if I get caught throwing it away---.

I'm trying to decide---shall I shave it off---or shall I leave it? Lots of pictures have been taken, but I still haven't seen any of them.

Radio is giving out news now. Seems I rate two stars on a ribbon, background of white and blue, the U.N. ribbon. Seems we also won a unit citation. I think there's also a third medal, but I'm not sure.

I don't like guard duty, but I also hope I don't get assigned to driving back there, either.


April 23, 1951. Chunchon. The Reds are doing their best to keep me from coming home. They made a break through our lines, the worst of which is just above us here. We've set up a defense perimeter, just in case. There isn't anything to worry about, though.

I still have no comment about MacArthur. He's still a newspaper hero to me.

Got paid tonight, an $85 check. I'll enclose it if I don't forget it. My mind isn't on what I'm doing these days. I might add the days are getting longer and longer. I don't look for them to discharge many Reserves right away. I hope, however, they'll let me out.

April 25, 1951. Chunchon. Everything's under control, except I talked too soon about going home. It's been canceled. Some of the men who were to be discharged on hardship and members of the brigade are still on their way, as of the last word.

The Reds have made a big push. Units have been moving back and we have word here the lines are holding. Guards were doubled last night and tonight. Even the Sgts. and SSgts. were walking post, including yours truly. Don't know how soon I'll get to leave for home, but it should be soon.

News reported the U.N. had closed the gap. The gap was just above us here. The main force of the push was against the Marine section. It was the ROKs who broke first. Then the U.S. Army pulled out, leaving their big guns in good condition with ammo. The Marines recaptured them from the Reds. That's the story I got, anyway. I know for a fact a number of the ROKs came through this area and got stopped and were shown the trail back.

They had to take it or else. Some were marching toward the front lines when I went to chow. ROKs are the South Korean Army.

One South Korean Marine was in to get spare parts and he was pretty much boiled over at the South Korean Army and didn't keep it a secret. He really blew his top. According to him, his unit is still in the lines and expect to stay there.

Of course you understand, Marines are Marines, regardless of the flag. I can't see getting into combat, but at the same time, I can't see running. If the boys in the lines need help-- well, what are we over here for? I might say I'm not the only one who feels that way. When we were told we were moving back, there was quite a roar that went up. So far we haven't moved although our gear is packed and ready. The 3rd platoon is at present with the 7th MT Bn. They moved back night before last. I don't know how far.

"Good Nite Irene" is on the radio. I've heard it before but not the way they sang it just now. "Sometimes she wears pajamas to bed, sometimes a nightgown, but when they're in the wash, she's the talk of the town."

Sgt. Newinhouse just poured water into my hot water on the stove (for me to wash in). He expected somebody, mostly Sam, to blow a fuse. He was standing there pouring it in and looking around from one to another, except me. When no one yelled at him, he looked at me, then turned red. I was looking nails at him.

"Is that your water, Pappy?" I knew what he was doing and don't care about the water; I'm not ready to use it yet anyway.

The news this evening sounds like double talk.


April 27, 1951. Hongchon. Everything's under control, except we're going backward instead of forward.

I'm first on the list for the next group to leave for the States, whenever that will be.

I could be wrong, but I don't believe they'll draft anyone for labor. Sounds like more rumors.

Nine o'clock news. Reds 11 miles from Seoul--40,000 Reds killed. We here in the tent want to know what they're doing with all the bodies. It doesn't seem to us there can be so many. U.N. seems to think they can hold at the Han River. At the rate they're going, it won't be possible. In fact, I look for us to move back still more. Most of us are for moving forward instead of back. I'm not the only one who has said out loud, "It looks like somebody has turned yellow." So much for that.

Yes, the officers wear the same combat clothes as the enlisted men. The only way you can tell the officers from the enlisted men are the bars on their collars and caps, if they are wearing them.  Not all enlisted men have stripes on their sleeves; it's sometimes confusing.

April 28, 1951.  Hongchon.  Haven't heard any more about me coming home.  We're expecting to move back some more in a few days.  This is a funny war.  Only I don't think anybody is laughing about it.

It's now 7:30.  It seems we don't have to work after supper any more for awhile.  Our working hours now are 7:45 to 11:30, 12:45 to 4:30.  We still don't get Sundays off.

Some western music on the radio now--excuse me--it's polka music.  Anyway, it sounds good.

Sgt. Sam Michich went to all the trouble to beg for a truck he could drive and pull the machine shop behind it.  Mr. Winn, the officer in charge, finally give in to him, providing I rode with him.  Of course, you understand I don't want to be assigned to driving a truck all the time, so I played dumb.  I just didn't know anything at all about driving a truck.  Every time I was asked a question about the truck, I just didn't know.  For example, I was asked if the tanks were full of gas.  I said I didn't know, which I really didn't, and I made them show me how to turn the switch and little buttons to check.  Anyway, Mr. Winn let Sam have an International truck just like the one I used to drive in the last war, except it had a cargo bed instead of a dump bed.  The engine was a brand new one.  It had just been installed and wasn't broken in. When Sam started up a steep hill, pulling the heavy machine shop (14 tons) behind, the engine got hot and stopped.  Sam got excited and it was necessary for yours truly to let go with what he knew about trucks--or jump.  On my side of the truck, it would mean a jump of some 50 feet straight down.  When the machine shop started pulling us back, I let go with what I knew about trucks instead of jumping.  I stopped the truck from rolling back down the grade, then we got two other trucks to tie on in front--both of them couldn't pull the truck and the machine shop up the hill.  We finally blocked the machine shop, unhitched it and hitched onto another truck with a regular driver who knew what he was doing and let him take it the rest of the way.

When we got the engine started again, Sam was driving about 30 miles an hour (20 is the speed limit) when we came to a narrow place in the road.  The road also curved, so we couldn't see far ahead.  I heard a noise up ahead and knew what it was. I didn't say anything.  I watched Sam and got ready to jump.  The ground was level on my side.  I laughed until my sides hurt when I saw Sam's face turn 14 different colors and his eyes bulge out like doughnuts. Sam had come face to face with a tank. The tank didn't slow down, but Sam did. He slammed on the brakes so hard I almost went out over the engine hood. My side of the truck was in the ditch when the tank took to the ditch on the other side, knocking down a tree. The tank kept going; it didn't even slow down. It took Sam a couple of minutes to get his breath and push his eyeballs back in place, while I sat and laughed. I think he could have shot me then. He said later he had wondered why I was watching him. When we got to the new area, Mr. Winn was waiting for us, laughing his head off. He had followed us part way in his jeep. The machine shop had beat us there. He looked at Sam, shook his head and laughed some more.

Mr. Winn was nobody's dummy. He knew I knew how to handle the truck if I wanted to.

May 1, 1951. Wonju. We moved last night. Sam and I made it in four hours without any trouble. We worked until midnight night before last. Worked until 4:30 yesterday when we were told to pack and move. We ate supper, packed our gear, and left at 6:00 and arrived at 10:00. I was told before we left to take over the driving by force it necessary, if Sam had any trouble what-so-ever. Only once he scared me. We had no brakes on the trailer and coming down this side of the pass, Sam wanted to use the brakes. He put his foot on the brake and I could feel the trailer sway. I could see the thing jack-knifing and taking off over the side, pulling us with it. I told him to take his foot off the brake. He didn't want to, but did anyway, and the truck and trailer straightened up and gained speed. We hit the curve at the bottom of the hill doing 90 to nothing. Every time Sam moved his foot, I yelled at him. He came through fine.

The men going home haven't left yet. I heard this morning they were due to leave in the morning. I'm still keeping my fingers crossed; I still may be on the list. I was called in day before yesterday to sign the "Fitness Report for Non-Commissioned Officers." It was different to what I had signed before. Only Sgts. on the list to go home were called in, so they said. But when I asked if I definitely was on the list, they didn't know. So there you are. Nobody wants to commit himself.

I'll be mighty glad when I can get out of here. I'm getting awfully tired of the messing around. These stupid people would run at the drop of a hat.

We here in the tent just pulled a dirty trick on one of the other Sgts. We planted a harmless dud beside his sack, a 105 mm shell that had been disarmed. I watched him walk over and even step right on it and he didn't see it. Then I got to writing this letter and didn't notice when he saw it. I'm sure I jumped at least three feet when he let out a scream, and then I watched him try to make a door in the side of the tent where there isn't any. He almost knocked over the tent. When he couldn't make a hole, he dived for the door and took off at high port. He stopped a long way off and yelled for us to get it out. I tried to get him to get a shovel and remove it. After all, it was by his sack. He said I was in the engineers and knew about those things and for me to get the lead out and remove it. He wouldn't come back until it was removed even though we told him we had planted it.

There's a formation at 7:30 in the morning. Our little radio is playing up a storm now. Band music. It's 9:30, the man says. Now Bob Hope at Camp Pendleton is on.


May 2, 1951. Wonju. It seems we were transferred back to the 10th Corps yesterday. We have been with the 8th Army since leaving Masan. I'm speaking of the entire division now. We were ordered back here by the 8th Army. Now it seems the 10th Corps wants us back up there. The 4th platoon left this morning to go back up to the same place we just came from. How about that? The rest of us expect to go back up at any time.

We're unable to do all the work necessary because of lack of parts. Of course they keep coming to the machine shop. You should see and hear about some of the stuff they ask us to do. Sometimes they ask us to perform miracles. I got news for you: sometimes we do. We've done what officers and staff have said was impossible. Maybe it takes two or three days, also working at night, but very seldom do we fail once we start something.


May 3, 1951. Wonju. Rates came out today and as far as I know, every Cpl. made Sgt. except one, and he made Cpl. less than a year ago. All Pfcs. except men newly arrived in the platoon made Cpl. I'm speaking only of the 2nd platoon. I don't know about the others except I hear they were about the same. There aren't enough in the lower ranks now to walk guard. So guess who will be walking post again.

It's 9:45 now. I stopped to listen to the news, shave, and drink some hot cocoa. They collected our oil heaters, so we don't have them to heat water any more. So--we pulled out our little gas stoves, found some gas (nearly all trucks and jeeps carry extra cans), and we heat our water, cocoa, coffee, etc. We found that two of us have stoves in this tent. We've been wondering what the driver says when he gets off some place miles from nowhere and finds he has no gas. Of course, a driver on his toes will check his cans before he leaves. It's hard to draw gas unless we have a jeep or truck to use it in. Of course Sam and I can get an extra can or two when the tanker fills the machine shop, so we don't have to steal it from the trucks.

May 5, 1951. Wonju. Was company Sgt. of the Guard last night. Six men for guard on two posts. Had to get up, wake the reliefs and post them. Didn't get much sleep; otherwise, everything's under control.

Some men are being changed around. A Sgt. Tate has been transferred from Shop platoon to 2nd platoon to take my place in the machine shop. He made Sgt. in this last promotion group. He used to do machine work on those expensive racers that make big names. In other words, he's a pretty good machinist. He joined the company at Hamhung. It'll be a little while before he'll be going home.

Hot cocoa is cooling. It's 9:45, and almost time for lights out. I hope the enlarging of the Marine Corps doesn't keep me in after I return to the States. I'm afraid it will, though. My enlistment isn't up until Dec. 8th, 1952. They can sure hold me.

May 6, 1951. Wonju. Everything's under control, except I'm getting homesick. Some more men went home today. I guess that's all now until the next list is made up, and I'm supposed to be near the top on it.

The battalion now at last has a shower. I went and took one this afternoon. It sure felt good.

The weather here is very nice right now. In fact, it's down right warm. We had a rain the other day and night, though, the night I was Sgt. of the Guard. Anyway, when I came in from work, I thought I was seeing things. Under my sack was a lake. We set up in a field and my cot straddles one of the furrows. One of the guys had said he ditched around the tent, but I should have checked to see how he did it. He had ditched so all the water from the tent would run into that furrow, and that's where my pack was. Luckily, the water didn't get inside and everything's okay. It pretty near burned me up, though. I had to go back out in the rain and drain the water off while those dopes laughed at me.

Put in for $40 cash this pay. It'll give me $66 in my pocket in case I see something I want to buy, which will be doubtful. There was $87 on the books. I still have $26 in my pocket. One thing about it, I could sure save money over here.

One truckload of replacements just came in. They said many more are on the way.

I asked one of the guys what I should write next and he said, "Tell her you just re-enlisted for six." One of the others wanted to know if he wanted the old man to get shot. I'm not about to re-enlist for six years or anything else, except maybe a lifetime in civilian status. If they keep bringing replacements in, maybe I'll make it yet. Rumor has May 15th down for the next group to go out.

We went on daylight savings time today. Lost an hour's sleep last night. Sure is lots of daylight after we get off of work at 5:30. We're working 7:45 to 5:30 now.

My watch is broken; the main spring, I think. I was just told it was 20 minutes to 9:00. It's just beginning to get dark. I'd better get my water on to shave, even if it doesn't take long for it to heat.

Another truckload of replacements came in. That's good. The plane that brings these in takes the others out. These men coming in look scared or worried. Wonder why.

Hot cocoa. Sgt. Newinhouse makes it every night. Tastes good.

May 7, 1951. Wonju. I just got moved into the staff tent. It seems they have too many Sgts., so to make room, they figured they could put up with me for the short time I would be here.

We went back to work after supper until 8 o'clock. I moved during that time and took as long as I could. In other words, I didn't do any work.

M/Sgt. Lisenberry said he rated 54 men in this platoon and he has 47.

They have a radio here, but I don't know if it works or not. I may have to go elsewhere to hear the news.

The radio works, and I just heard the news. The Top is passing around the word that lights are to stay on until 11. Just finished shaving, so now to finish this and hit the sack.

A surprising number of men are re-enlisting in the Regulars. I'm surprised at some of the Reserves. They're the very ones who have been howling the loudest.

May 10, 1951. Wonju. We got another man assigned to the machine shop, Pvt. Sutter. That makes four of us now. With the work light now anyway, we're having a picnic. Sam and I are ready to retire. I retired once. Went into the tent and got my clothes good and wet and was soaping them down when Mr. Winn entered the tent. "Oh, there you are. I got some work for you," he said, and he un-retired me.

May 12, 1951. Wonju. I haven't heard much more than rumors about going home. Some of the officers were telling around this morning that not all the Inchon men would be out before Sept. 1st. I just smiled, because I remembered I had number 1 and am supposed to be on the next list. I quit smiling when I heard the 9:00 news. Marines are making a lot of staff Sgts. out of buck Sgts. Several thousand of them, in fact. The announcement in itself doesn't mean a lot to me, but it made me recall some remarks made to me within the last two weeks. Remarks I took for so much hogwash, but now I'm wondering. These remarks have been made only by staff and above. "If you made staff, it would pay you to stay in the Corps." "you're not going home. You're staying over here until we go." The staff has already been told there is no plan to send them home. An officer: "You're not going home. You're staying over here." I told him if I wasn't on the next list I was going to make a lot of noise. He just laughed; I took it as a joke.

Another officer: "You know why you were taken off the last list, don't you?" Speaking before thinking, I said sure, "It was because there were too many hardship cases." He shook his head and laughed, "You're not going home for a while." He left me with my face hanging out, staring at his back as he walked away.

I don't think their remarks mean anything more than just jokes, but there must be some reason for them. Anyway, I don't think there was a more useless person in this unit than I was yesterday and today. Maybe my trying to do the right thing has been my undoing. Anyway, I'm proud of the small advancement I have been able to make in the Marines. I'm still going to consider all the remarks as jokes until I find out different but I can't help wondering.

May 14, 1951. Wonju. We were secured at 2 P.M. because of it being Mother's Day. It surprised us all. We weren't warned ahead of time. Everyone was so dazed they just sacked out. I relaxed and read an adventure story in back China. Can you fancy that? It was a search for a jade mountain. Now don't laugh at me, durn it.

Instructions for servicemen concerning the treatment of the replacements coming in: "Give him the best of everything, even to giving him your sleeping bag, but by all means don't let him get away."

Have you heard the song, "Rotation Blues?" It's pretty good.

Someone found some boxing gloves somewhere and

after supper tonight some of the men showed off.  Only one showed any training.  I do believe I could have done better than most of them.  I kept my distance anyway.  After all, I'm not mad at anybody.  I don't want to put them in the hospital.  Har-har.

It seems there's to be a list of men to go home in the next group come out no later than the 20th.  I should be somewhere near the top.  I hope.


May 16, 1951.  Wonju.  It's been raining and this evening it's a bit chilly.  Due to the rain, the planes can't land, so they tell me, and we can't get any mail.


May 17, 1951.  Wonju.  There still is no news on my going home.  I am hoping to be able to leave here by the 1st of June anyway, but one can never tell.

The Reds broke through again.  Again it was the ROKs that broke.  Was told the 5th and 7th Marines received a heavy jolt.  Tanks, trucks and troops moving heavy all day.  The 4th platoon pulled in a few minutes ago.  It's almost 9:30 P.M.  that still leaves the 3rd platoon up there somewhere.  They're with 7th MT.  Troops on the move include both Marines and Army.

I wasn't sure I'd get to write tonight.  I washed some clothes in addition to going out after supper and working a little while.  I even got myself shaved already and I'm trying to figure out how I did it so I can keep it up.  I took off from work this afternoon and took a shower and put on clean clothes.

One of the men Sam and I are breaking in in the machine shop, Pvt. Sutter, is 24 years old.  He has done this type of work before.  He's married, has one child with another on the way.  He was doing a lot of figuring in the shop the other day and when I asked what the figures were for, he told me about his family.  He was trying to figure out just how he could fit in a hospital bill.  I didn't know what to tell him, other than to go and see the Chaplain.  That's just what he did.  I don't know what happened.

Three of the staff are in the sack now, and the other one is getting ready, so I suppose I'll have to close.  The lights to give us a chance to write letters.  The staff can come in during the day and write while the rest of us can't.  They don't say anything to me for keeping the lights on, but they turn over, look at the light, then look at me, then look at their watches, then turn their backs on the light and a few minutes later the whole thing again.  I'd just as soon they told me to put the light out.  In the morning, little remarks will be made about not being able to get me out of the sack.  "He stays up late and sleeps late."  Oh, well--they'll be sorry when I'm gone.

May 21, 1951. Wonju. Everything's under control. Rumor has it 66 men will leave from battalion about June 2nd or 3rd, 14 from this company: the eight who were on the list and were taken off, plus six others. This sounds pretty much correct, although I haven't received it officially. One date I heard also was May 27th. I'll try to talk to the Top Sgt. tomorrow and see what I can find out for sure. He usually screams and yells at anybody asking questions, although he hasn't treated me in that manner. He's always treated me with respect. Except for a few yardbirds, everybody has. It's sure been different this time from last. I had a hard time getting used to it. In fact, I've had a hard time getting used to this war altogether.

Fredette--I didn't think I'd ever run into anybody else with that name. I saw it printed on the back of a guy's jacket and I asked him about it. He not only said it was his family name, but it was a very popular French family name. [Fred's youngest daughter's middle name is Fredette.]

Shortly after chow, I was called in with four other men so the Captain could give us a pep talk. It seems, according to him, we are the only five Reserves going home out of 23 men from this company. All the others are Regulars. Anyway, the pep talk was to get us to ship over into the Regulars. Also (and here is the pay-off), we are subject to 21 months of extended active duty, or until the end of the enlistment date, whichever comes first. My enlistment is up Dec. 8th, 1952. The inactive Reserves are to be released first. Then the organized Reserves have been divided into five different classes. He didn't know how the classes were made up or how a man was chosen for any certain class. He used the word release most. However, he did say that when a man was discharged, he was subject to call for the next ten years following, regardless of whether he was a member of the Reserve or not.

I started to say if I had to stay in the Corps another 11 months, I might as well stay over here, but I checked myself. I have a feeling I'll be able to get released. Could be wrong of course. Anyway, what the Captain said is what he said, whether it's right or wrong. He said he wasn't telling us all that stuff because he wanted to, but because he had received a direct order to do so. And we are to be called in later to sign a statement to the effect he had told it to us. He admitted he didn't even know what the enlisted men's pay was. As a matter of fact, he didn't know much of anything, except that he was a Reserve himself and he had lost his business when he was called in. He thought anyone who signed up with the Reserves or Regulars needed his head examined.  Some pep talk.  I sat and looked at a candid snapshot book while he talked.  The other guys laughed most of the time.  Some pretty good shots in the book--yes, there really were.

No one knows for sure when we'll leave here.  There's five out of my platoon going.  So far, that is.  That will make Sam No. 1 for next time.

After supper tonight when we went back out to work, I sat down on a barrel of gas that was turned on its side, and that's where I was later when Mr. Winn came along.  He looked at me, then turned to M/Sgt. Linsenberry and pointed at me.  "They might just as well to have sent him home the last time.  He hasn't done a damned thing since the group left."

I said, "You're so damned right and I ain't about to do anything either."  He came over and sat on the barrel beside me. We talked about this and that.  I wouldn't have gotten up and gone to work if I lost all three stripes.  After a while, he left.  I then noticed I was sitting on the barrel in the middle of the compound all by myself.  Everyone had secured.  So I went back to the tent, too.

These guys think I should wear the mustache home.  It fits me, they say.

May 25, 1951. Wonju.  I left here this morning with some others at 7:30 and went to Chunchon where we picked up some new trucks and trailers.  Not new, either, but rebuilt.  I drove one of them back. It was all right, except it was very dusty.  I made it though, without a bit of trouble.  Got back here about 2 P.M. We didn't have to work after supper this evening.  There is or was some kind of Korean show up by the Chaplain's tent.  I didn't go up, so don't know just what it was.

It seems we can't print the address any more.  We have to write it.  How about that?  I can't write good.

I got tired of trying to trim my mustache, so I shaved it off last night.  "Afraid to let your wife see it?"  "Hell, you look plum naked."  "Hey, Pappy, you look 10 years younger."  Well, that's how it is.

Was told this afternoon buck Sgts. can now be promoted to staff by company commander if they have held the grade for at least one year (12 months).  Up to this time, it was 18 months and the warrant came only from Washington.

The young guys who are now holding Sgt. or Cpl. and stay in the Corps will really make out if they increase the size of the Corps.  I'm a civilian at heart, but I'm afraid the increase in the size of the Corps, if approved, will make it harder for me to get out.

Was just told the list of men going home is on the HQ bulletin board. My name is in group one of three groups. They said the officers were listed also, but they weren't interested enough to see who they were. I'll have to go up in the morning and see the list for myself. The date given is approximately the 3rd of June.


May 28, 1951. Wonju. We're all alone now, just the 2nd platoon, four guys in auto supply and about six or eight in Headquarters including two cooks and a corpsman. Not only that, but we aren't at all busy. It's been raining heavy and we had to set up another tent. I had charge of the detail. We also moved the head a little closer.

I moved into the tent myself with four other Sgts. This morning I had charge of the detail that moved the three tents of the galley and all their gear down closer. We were supposed to have moved it two days ago, but the heavy rains prevented it. The day the rest of the battalion moved up, it was raining hard and we were very glad we didn't have to move.

The password for tonight is pine-tree, the guard just told us.

I don't think you need to worry about me getting very close to the fighting. I'm not about to go up to the front lines, although a few times the lines have come back on me.

It's 9:55: I've just five minutes to finish this. Sgt. Tate now turns out the lights at 10:00, as we are again using the machine shop generator for lights. There goes the warning flicker. I'm smart, I am. I let Tate have the keys before he realized what it meant. I'm getting lazy, I guess, maybe. It could be. Oh, well.


May 31, 1951. Wonju. New date for departure is June 15th. I've been taken off group 1. As far as I could find out, only Reserves were taken off. The Regulars are still on the list, except for those in group 3, and all of those are off. The excuse is that all Reserves are ordered out by July 1st and they want them all to go at the same time. They are all to be discharged as soon as they reach the States. Pardon me, but it stinks.

We're only about 12 miles from the airfield. The company is about 60 miles away. It would seem logical the men going home would come here. I don't know what their plans are.

There isn't enough work now to keep us busy. We either read or sleep. That's me. Some play cards or just argue about anything they happen to think of. Anyway, we're getting some much needed rest.  Maybe I should say the others needed it.  I haven't done anything to need rest.

June 1st. 1951. Wonju.  Everything's under control.  I've been ordered to pack my gear and leave in the morning.  I've still got my fingers crossed.  I've got Sgt. of the Guard tonight.

Mr. Winn told me to get ready to go.  He didn't say just where I was to go.  MSgt. Lisenberry went up to the company today to get the straight scoop.

I have to pack my gear now, but I don't think it'll take me long.  Chow over--no mail.

It seems we go up to the company and are supposed to take the plane to Hongchon.

Florence, Ethel, Louella Mae, 1951

June 2, 1951.  Chunchon.  Well, here I am with the company. There were four of us who came up, but one went back.  On other words, there are three of us to go home from the 2nd platoon, but nobody knows when.  Anyway, we had 65 miles of dust to go through, and what do you know?  I was in charge of the convoy. Of course there were only two trucks and a jeep, but it was new to me.  One truck lost its brake fluid.  Going over these passes without brakes ain't funny.  Almost lost the other truck when a tank that was being trailed (towed) behind another swung out in front of him.  I'm sure he didn't miss it by the breadth of a hair.  I was riding the jeep in the lead.  The way that thing was swinging all the way across the road made me think my two trucks would have a slim chance.  I looked back just in time to see it swing right at the truck, and my hair stood on end.  The other truck missed it when it swung the other way.  One track was off the tank and there was no one steering it.  I'm sure surprised no one got hurt.

The jeep I was in had a defect.  Every time we got up to 20 miles per hour, the tailend would swing.  I didn't check to see what the trouble was until I got here.  I'm glad I didn't.  If I had, I'm sure I'd have gotten out and walked.  The only thing holding the rear axle was the springs; the brackets were broken.

Lights out at 10:00, and I'm told it's three minutes till. They're a bit cranky.  It seems we're a little close to the fighting. Anyway, that's what they say.

June 3, 1951.  Chungchon.  The Top just called me and gave me the pills for me and my two men that we have to take every Sunday.  That's how I know when Sunday comes around.

June 4, 1951.  Chunchon.  Everything's under control...I think.  As of this date and time, 6:30 P.M., we are to leave the battalion CP (command post) at 8:00 A.M. the 6th.  All Regulars were taken off the list and Reserves put in their place.  The Regulars are burned up.  I don't blame them, in a way.  Some of the Reserves just got here and are going back.  It means the Regulars will be here for a while yet.

Unless the orders are changed again, I'll be on my way in a couple of days.  This has been very confusing.  I am living right in the company office tent.  You know what that means.  Keep my mouth shut, my eyes and ears open---.

They were taking all the Reserves off the list when the

order came in about an hour before noon to take the Regulars off. Talk about surprises---.

I took a detail over and helped Bob Wilson fix up the movie area yesterday. Then it rained last night. I hope it doesn't rain again tonight--would like to see the movie. It rained a couple of hours this afternoon.

Rumor has it the Division is going back to Masan until it can get back up to strength.

Oh, boy, I bet I was on and off the list a dozen times yesterday. I was so confused I couldn't even begin to write last night. Both of the men who came up with me day before yesterday were taken off. One of them found out he was a Sgt. when he got here. The other one is also a Sgt. Both are Regulars, and very mad. Of course all the Regulars are blaming the Reserves as though it was their fault. I thought sure there would be a riot this afternoon here in the tent.


June 5, 1951. Chunchon. I leave at 0800 tomorrow. There are only three of us from this company in the first group. I've an idea I'll be home by July 1st or shortly after.

They changed things on the rest of the Reserves again. Only the men called to active duty on or before July 31st are to go back to the States. I and the others in groups 1 and 2 are going on the regular rotation system. Group 1 leaves tomorrow morning and group 2 tomorrow evening. The other Reserves go on standby on the 8th and will leave any time after.

It makes a lot of sense. It's as clear as mud to me.

The company is moving on up about eight miles tomorrow. I won't see the other place. I have to go back as far as Hoengsong and take a plane for Pusan. My first plane ride. I'm looking forward to it.


June 8, 1951. Pusan. I'm on my way. All my gear has been turned in. I drew a set of dungarees. Turned change of address cards in and now there's nothing more to do until we board the boat for Japan. We're to turn in our sleeping bags and mess gear before we board ship. My group goes aboard the morning of the 10th. We're to be in Kobe, Japan, about two days and then to the States.

The airplane ride was quite the stuff--like riding in a car on a smooth, paved highway, except when we came in for the landing. My ears started hurting and my right one hurt right on down into my neck and shoulder. It was all right in a few minutes after my feet hit the ground. The bad cold I have may have caused it.

I have two different kinds of pills and a bottle of stuff I have to take every so many hours. I went to the Army sick bay after we got here and the guy handed the stuff right out as soon as I told him what was wrong. I already feel better.

There were 40 of us on the plane, a big four motor job. Looking down on the ground from way up there was just like pictures I have seen.

June 14, 1951. Aboard Sgt. S. Analak

Aboard ship, approximately 8000 miles from San Diego. Master's noon report describes the sea as moderate. In my way of thinking, it's a little rough. Sitting on a ladder with my writing pad on my knee.

I've been trying to figure out how to write a letter of interest that has a good chance of arriving after I do. Perhaps I should start where I left off with my last letter written in Pusan.

We were deloused. Turned in our gear except dungarees, socks, underwear, and other personal items such as shaving gear.

We were told we didn't have liberty in Pusan. A large number of men took off anyway. Army M.P.s brought them back by the truckload. I heard of only one they turned in, however. He didn't come with us. We were able to go as far as the Red Cross where they had the only showers I could find. They also had free coffee and donuts.

We were allowed to keep the bottom part of our pack or the waterproof bag we kept our sleeping bags in, for our personal gear. I found the pack wouldn't hold all my personal gear, so I kept both, the pack and the bag. When we were ready to leave, I put the pack inside the bag, which of course looked pretty full. I couldn't see throwing good gear away that I might need.

There was no shakedown and no one paid any attention to me.

The boat trip from Pusan to Kobe was uneventful. I was put on one clean-up detail, but didn't do much.

Things didn't work out so well when we arrived in Kobe. We were to have liberty as soon as we could get our seabags and get on khaki uniforms. The liberty was to be until midnight, and that was all we were to get. I wasn't bothered, because I could do everything I wanted to do in one evening anyway.

A detail of Japs was bringing sea bags to the dock where we were. Not all the sea bags showed up, including mine. After waiting around for some time, we got permission to go look for our bags in the warehouse where they were stored. An officer went along with us. After looking all over the place for the bag I knew was well marked, I started looking at each tag. It took time. Sure enough, my tag was on a brand new sea bag. No lock. A Marine Corps hand seal. I had to sign for the bag before they would let me break the seal. I didn't want somebody else's seabag, so while an officer looked on, I shoved my fist between the folds to the enclosure and pulled out, of all things, my own rubber stamp. The officer explained my bag must have busted open and the contents were dumped into a new bag.

After signing for it, I opened it and dumped it out just outside the warehouse. My hand bag was gone. Blanket, all my pipes, as well as several other items, were gone. I was surprised to see the iron was still there. All the uniforms were still there. The briefcase I had my lessons and books in had been opened and the contents dumped out. Nobody needs to tell me how the bag got busted. I know. A zipper on the briefcase like that couldn't open up by itself. I was pretty much burned up by the time I got back to the ship, only to find I had been put on guard duty and was to go on post at 4 o'clock. I hadn't had lunch. It was well past lunch time.

I went to the mess hall. They weren't feeding and weren't going to until the following morning. I found out it was a quarter till 4. I didn't know where the Guard office was, and nobody I asked knew either or at least didn't want anybody to know they knew. Almost everyone aboard were men that had been with me looking for their seabags.

On the way out of the mess hall, I was bumped into from behind. I turned in time to see three Marines duck into the scullery. One of them had something under his dungaree jacket. I thought if that was food, I wanted some of it. The last guy started to close the door, but found he couldn't. I was standing in the way. He looked at me and said, "Come on in." I went. We had finished and hidden the pan when the head cook, a civilian, came in. He looked at us with surprise. "What the hell are you birds doing in here? Get out of here before I put you to work." We went, but fast. That apple pie sure was good.

I figured it must be pretty near 4 o'clock and they can do things to a person for not showing up for guard. On my way down a passage, I saw the guard relief being posted. I knew them by the M.P. bands on their arms. A Sgt. had been assigned Cpl. of the Guard. Of course he didn't know me from Adam when I walked up and asked him. "What goes?" He took a lot for granted and told me, with a short oath, I had been secured and to shove off.

While I changed my clothes, I tried to figure out where I was to check out to leave the ship. No one I asked knew. Those who weren't going ashore didn't care and those that were had already gone.

I learned at this time we were to pick up some more men here in Kobe and they had already come aboard. They were the ones on guard.

I found some sheets by the compartment hatchway, but they were the wrong ones. They were for corpsmen only. I headed for the gangplank. I figured the sentry there would stop me, but he didn't even look at me. I guess he was too busy trying to hide the cigarette he was smoking. I went down the gangplank onto the dock, crossed the warehouse and went out the exit where I found myself in a yard with a gate at the one end. It was easy to see it was the gate I was to go through. It was pretty well covered by M.P.s, both Marine and Army, as well as some special Jap police. As this was the only gate, I approached sure I would be asked for a pass. They surprised me by turning their backs and I walked through the gate without any problem.

The street I found myself on reminded me a great deal of China, but it was cleaner. I had never been in downtown Kobe before. I didn't know what to expect. I had hoped I would be able to go with one of the other fellows who knew his way around, but was going only for the purpose of doing some shopping like myself. However, I was alone with ricksha boys, peddlers, beggars, merchants, newsboys, taxi drivers, storekeepers or their employees, and geisha girls, all pulling at me. Each was trying to get me to be a customer. I soon found out it was easy to get rid of them. All I had to do was show them my American money. They shied away from it like it was poison. I had no "yen" and they would have nothing to do with me until I had changed my money. I didn't know where to change my American dollars to the coin of the realm. I walked down the street that seemed the most popular from the docks. I couldn't read the Jap street signs, so I kept looking back, trying to imprint certain buildings or street features on my mind so I could find my way back.

By this time, my mind was pretty well mixed up. (The boat is pitching, my legs are cramping, and I'm about to fall off this ladder. I'm writing this letter in great detail, but then I've nothing else to do. It'll soon be supper time.)

Wandering on down the street, I began to wonder, what was I going to buy? What could I find in this town my little family would like? Right away I thought of two things that were against me. At least I thought so at the time. First, it couldn't cost too much, because I didn't have too much to spend. Second, it couldn't be too bulky or I wouldn't be able to carry it with me. Some of the men I knew were planning on mailing their items home.  But after buying what I wanted, I felt I wouldn't have enough money left over to pay the mailing charges.  Yes, but what did I want?  I didn't know.

They had told us that once we had changed American money for "yen," we couldn't change it back again.  I figured I could buy $20 worth of "yen" or 7,200.  Then I wondered, what were the prices like?  I looked in a display window I was passing. It was full of collector's pipes. Oh, brother: 12,000 yen for a pipe I couldn't even smoke?  Anyway, my family wouldn't care for that.

I had walked only a short distance when I realized someone had stopped in front of me.  Before I could stop or dodge to one side, we had bumped together.  I found myself staring into a face with a smiling mouth showing nice shiny buck teeth, spotted with gold.  The black-rimmed glasses set off his round face.

For a minute I thought I was back on Okinawa on a certain afternoon, but that's another story.

I took the piece of paper he was handing me and read about the store I was standing in front of.  I showed him my money and he motioned me inside, continuing to smile.  I thought now maybe I was getting somewhere.  Maybe they would exchange my money in there.  I started in, then stopped.  I remembered the warning we had been given aboard ship about going into off-limits areas.  I looked the whole front over and couldn't find any signs I could read.  I went in.

There were some other Marines in there.  They didn't have any yen either and didn't know where to get it.  They were just as lost as I was.  Since they didn't seem to care for my company, I didn't press it.

I assumed the clerk would go to them first, but he came to me. I showed him my money.  He explained to me in very good English that they weren't permitted by law to exchange or accept American money.  It would be necessary for me to go to the OSS and exchange it.  It was a little store, but rather neat.  The clerk went to a desk in a corner and got a map.  He showed me where to go.  I had some more walking to do.

When I hit the sidewalk again, there was another Marine with his face about three inches from the Jap's.  It was plain to see his horrified expression and the sweat running down his face. Finally, he reached out and took the paper, glanced at it, giggled, and went into the store.  I wondered if I had looked so silly.

(Supper over and I'm now in the mess hall at a table.)

I followed direction and came to a tall building before reaching the elevated railway.  Outside was a sign:  "OSS," 6th floor.  I found the entrance, pushed on the swinging doors, and went in. Talk about surprises: The clerks were Jap and the signs were all in Japanese, but otherwise it was just like walking into the May Co., Woolworth's or a J.C. Penney store. Stocked the same way; arranged the same. Everything from cheap fountain pens to expensive fur coats were for sale. I moved across the floor as I looked and finally found myself at the bottom of a stairway. A sign stated: "OSS, 6th floor." It was the only sign I could see in English. I wondered what OSS meant. I never did find out.

I went up the stairs to find a little sign on each floor, "OSS 6th floor." I looked around on each floor, though. One floor had nothing but yard goods of different kinds. Another had ladies' ready-to-wear. Another had children's and still another had men's ready-to-wear, etc.

I got to the 6th floor and found a long line of Marine and Navy personnel. I got in line. Then I noticed the four elevators nearby.

It didn't take me too long to get to the window. A sign above it informed us the little office was under the supervision of the Bank of America. I got my 7,200 yen and thought I might as well start my shopping right in this store. However, the clerks avoided me, and I bought absolutely nothing. Perhaps I used the wrong approach.

Back on the sidewalk, I stared into the display windows as I walked along. They had different items of interest. Whole sets of dishes caught my attention. I went in and asked the price; went on down the street. I was still thinking about the dishes when I noticed a camera on display. I had wanted a camera and this one was the right size, no larger than a package of cigarettes. The price tag was 850 yen. I looked at the sun. It would get dark around 9:00. I didn't know what time it wa, since my watch was broken. I figured if I expected to get any pictures though, I'd better get at it. As I went through the door of the little shop, I wondered if I would be able to buy a new watch here. There certainly wouldn't be time to get my broken one repaired.

I bought the camera. The little man was quite excited about the 4.5 lens, although it meant nothing to me. He even gave me a little leather carrying case for it. I then asked for a couple boxes of film. I don't know why I asked for boxes instead of rolls, but it was just as well. I wouldn't have gotten just two rolls anyway. They came six rolls to one box, 10 exposures to a roll.

I got outside, found myself a corner by a building, and started sweating. Loading that camera was worse than trying to thread a needle on a crowded street. The camera is small, the film is small, and my fingers are too large. It hadn't occurred to me to have the little man load it for me.  After a great deal of strange struggle, I finally got it loaded.

I started looking for something to take pictures of that I would like to show back home.  I hadn't realized what I was in for when I started sporting a brand new camera on the street.  It meant "yen."  The first thing I knew, I had a giggling girl on each arm.  I had let them pull me a little way before I caught on.  When I saw they were dragging me into any alley, I jerked free of them.  The people on the street started laughing at me.  Oh, brother, I took off at high port.  They weren't bad looking girls, though.  American clothes, lipstick, well, all the proper trimmings and such.

I finally ended with one roll of film before it got dark.  Then I couldn't get the roll of film out of the camera.  I remembered a pair of tweezers I had aboard ship.  I left it go until later when I found that the tweezers worked fine.

One of the pictures I got was of the neat little stores under the elevated railway.  I wonder why the same thing couldn't be done under our viaducts.  I walked through these little stores.  It was all right.  Like going through the home show at city auditorium.  Each merchant had his own little stall.  Some large, some small.  All glassed in, clean and neat.

By this time it was getting pretty dark, and I was afraid to wander too far.  I wasn't about to get lost and miss the boat sailing for the States the next morning.

I found my way back to the little store I'd been in first.  Bought a few little items that maybe my little family will be able to say, "Daddy brought them from Japan."  While leaving there, I walked off down a side street I'd taken a picture of earlier and found another item which I bought for my wife.

I had a thousand yen left.  But I couldn't find anything I could see any sense to buying for a thousand yen, except what I had already bought.  Then I found a store with a watch for 4,000 yen and other items I could buy and bring home.  I could see some use to them and I would be able to carry them.  I almost ran back to the OSS building to get some more yen--wouldn't you know--they were closed.

I didn't think any more about going back to the place with the watch.  Walking toward the ship, I passed the store where I had bought the camera.  I got to thinking, would it be possible to buy film for the little camera in the States?  I went back and bought five boxes of film.

The M.P.s just glanced at me as I went through the gate and onto the ship.  I was asleep as soon as I hit the sack.

I felt much better the following morning when I went up

on deck to see men still coming up the gang plank even though liberty had expired at midnight.  Four Marines and two civilian crew members hadn't shown up when the ship sailed.

While I was watching the men come aboard, I got to thinking about the day before.  I could remember seeing things I could have brought along.  I thought then and even now, I could have gone back and gotten enough yen while I could and bought such things as albums with dragon designs and silk tablecloths. The didn't cost too much and I could have brought them with me very easily.

I don't know why I didn't go get enough yen and buy such items.  I had come back to the ship with $42 still in my pocket. My little family is worth every penny I had in my pocket.  I had spent just $20 and a big part of that on myself.  I don't know how to explain it, but I feel guilty as hell.

About four days out from Kobe, the water got rough.  It rained and the wind blew.  I got sick.  It was cold up there.  I still don't feel good even though the weather and water have quieted down.  I don't expect to feel good until I get off the rocking tub.

Two days ago I was on a cleaning detail.  I didn't do anything except watch the others do the work.

Last night I was put on guard.  This time (rocky-a-by-baby) I was Cpl. of the Guard.  The guard on this boat has been rather mixed up.  I've even seen staffs standing post.  I posted three of four Sgts. on my relief.  It was while on guard that I caught the writing bug.  I was in the troop personnel office when a guy who was writing at a desk turned and asked me to read the report he had been writing and tell him what was wrong with it. He knew something was wrong, but couldn't find it.

I didn't, of course, know who he was.  He was wearing a shirt with Sgt.'s stripes.  I didn't say anythIng.  I read the report, then surprised myself as well as him as to the number of things I remembered about news writing.  I corrected a number of things in the item and he agreed I was right.  He went on writing.  I leaned over and looked at some of the other items on the desk. They were all news reports on things happening aboard ship.  I asked him what those were for.  Oh, he was a war correspondent. That one item was going to the <u>Leatherneck</u>.  He was also a foreign correspondent for the Associated Press and--I left to check my sentries.  I never learned his name.

About a week ago, I saw a guy in the head with two watches on his arm.  I asked why he thought it necessary to wear two watches.  He explained he had loaned $22.50 on it and got stuck.  I offered him $20 for it and got myself a 17-jewel watch with a metal band just like mine, except with a different name.

It's almost 11:00 o'clock and I hear the fresh water showers are on, so---.

June 25, 1951.  There's been a lot of talk about the Reserves, pro and con, getting discharges, etc.  I'm returning under the rotation system.  The other Reserves aboard are under different orders, which I missed by one day.  I was called to active duty Aug. 1st. All of these men were called before July 31st.  All have been processed here aboard ship.

I got up my nerve and walked into the Sgt/Maj's office like I owned the place, sat down, and started asking questions.  I figured they would kick me out, but they were very nice and I believe they tried to give me the straight dope as they knew it. The persons who are to receive discharges are those whose enlistments are up or can't pass their physicals.  They didn't think there would be very many.  The Reserves on regular rotation weren't processed because there's no authorization to do so. According to the information they had, I would be processed as soon as I got off the ship or one month later, after my furlough, depending on how crowded they were in San Diego.  I may or may not know my next assignment when I left for my furlough. However, it's more than possible I'll receive an assignment to inactive duty before I leave on furlough.  There it is, straight as I could get if from the horse's mouth.

I'm sitting on a stair landing inside the hatch off the bow where the wind won't blow my paper overboard.  I can't smoke in the hold and the head is no place to write.

I've almost given up smoking.  It hasn't tasted right since I left Kobe.  Of course, I was looking forward to smoking the good pipes I had in my sea bag.  I was pretty much disgusted when I couldn't find them.

This ship is a converted freighter, not at all ideally arranged to carry troops.  There's about 1000 sacks and about 1400 of us aboard.  Cots have been set up any place where one would fit, including the recreation area.

There's only six fresh water showers when they're on. They were turned on for the first time yesterday.  There's lots of salt water, which leaves a person sticky.

The mess hall is small, but they've been serving good meals.  Movies have been shown every night, In the recreation area, which is below deck, there are books, games, etc., that can be checked out.

The ship's chaplain holds services in the recreation area every Sunday.  He also, with the help of the special services officer, puts out a daily news sheet to let us know what's going on.

The ship is operated by the Military Sea Transport Service. The crewmen are civilians (Civil Service), not union.

We've passed one ship since leaving Kobe.

The other night there was a bright light off to the North. We never did find out what it was, but it looked just like the sunrise early in the morning, It was 2 A.M.

According to the order we've received so far on getting off the ship, there's little chance any of us will be able to use a telephone right away. The nearest of kin of the men living within 150 miles of San Diego have been notified of the ship's arrival.

I was planning on writing a letter in Kobe giving the arrival place and time, but they didn't tell us until we had left the dock. We're supposed to dock the 27th and go off the ship at noon.


June 29, 1951. San Diego, Calif. I understand we can expect to leave here Wednesday. We go on schedule Monday. In the meantime, we have liberty if we want it. Most everyone is gone. I have nothing to go into San Diego for unless it's to see a show, and I can see one right here if I want to pay the enormous price of 12¢.

I've been thinking it might be best to take a plane after all. It may cost more, but it would get me there sooner. [He came by train.]

Most of these guys here have the idea they're going to get a discharge. I hope we do, but a few like myself think they will assign us to inactive duty and maybe even extend the enlistment time.

I was hoping I would be able to get home for the fourth, but it looks like that's out now.

The ribbons I bought in Denver have been outlawed. They're 1/8" too wide. I might have to buy the new narrow ones. They frown on a guy for not wearing them. They're worn right on the shirt now with emblems on the shirt collar. Had to buy a set of emblems, one for each side of the field scarf or tie (60¢).

I only have one set of Sgt. stripes. I've been trying to get some more so I can get a shirt ready for the homeward trip. I can wear dungarees part of the time, but the uniform of the day is khaki and it's the only way to get into the PX or movie and other places.

Arrived home July 5th, 1951.
(Was placed on inactive duty.)
Received discharge Dec., 1952.

I.      Endnotes for Korean War Section:

1.      U.S. Dept. of State. <u>Background notes: South Korea.</u> Washington, D.C.: GPO, 1987.

2.      Parker, William D. <u>A Concise History of the United States Marine Corps, 1775-1969.</u> Washington, D.C.: Historical Division, Headquarters, United States Marine Corps, 1970, pp. 79-87.

3.      Nakkula, Al. "Families Weep as Denver Marines Entrain." <u>Rocky Mountain News</u> 3 Aug. 1950, p. 5.

4.      Griffin, William J.K. "Typhoon at Kobe." <u>Marine Corps Gazette</u>, Sept., 1951, pp. 60-65.

5.      Personnel record for Fred T. Klemm, USMCR.

6.      Interview with the author.

7.      Montross, Lynn, and Nicholas A. Canzona. <u>U.S. Marine Operations In Korea 1950-1953, vol. II: The Inchon-Seoul Operation</u>. Washington, D.C.: Historical Branch, G-3, Headquarters U.S. Marine Corps, 1955.

8.      -----. <u>U.S. Marine Operations in Korea 1950-1953, vol. III: The Chosin Reservoir Campaign</u>. Washington, D.C.: Historical Branch, G-3 Headquarters U.S. Marine Corps, 1957, pp. 27-31.

9.      Hastings, Max. <u>The Korean War</u>. NY: Simon & Schuster, 1987, p. 152.

10.      Montross, vol. 3, pp. 244-45.

11.      Truman, Harry S. "Radio and Television Report to the American People on the National Emergency, December 15,1950." <u>Public Papers of the Presidents of the United States: Harry S. Truman...January 1 to December 31, 1950</u>. Washington, D.C.: GPO, 1965, pp. 741-46.

12.    Millett, Allan R. <u>Semper Fidelis, the History of the United States Marine Corps</u>. NY: Macmillan, 1980, p. 496.

Cpl. Fred T. Klemm, 1950 or 1951

II.	Editor's comments:

My only clear memory of World War II is of my dad coming home. I was older (eight) when my dad left for Korea, and I remember that well. Probably not enough is said or written about the families of combat troops. My sister and I worried and prayed that Dad would come home safely; Mother had that worry--that he might not come home--plus the additional worries and responsibilities of taking care of bills, food, house, car, and the raising of their daughters. And, of course, she had all those same problems (except for the car) and worries in World War II, when my sister and I were younger.

Of course the best memory (for me) of the Korean War was Christmas, July 5, 1951. I can remember some sort of a table-top artificial tree, but I don't remember setting it up before going to the train station to get Daddy. I asked Mother about that recently. She replied that my sister and I refused to let her take it down after Christmas in December! Even though the faculty and staff of Dad's school (Washington Park Elementary, Denver) had made sure we had a real tree and gifts for Christmas, we couldn't celebrate fully without Dad. We loved the fans and scarves he brought from Japan, and we were fascinated by what we called his "spy camera." (It did upset me to read in his notes that he felt guilty about not buying more for us. All we really wanted was him!)

Dad hasn't talked about his combat experience very much, but I do remember a few stories he has told through the years. He has had several strokes and he doesn't remember as much as he used to. But when we where going through pictures for this book, I asked a few questions.

Q:	"What was the incident about you knocking your tent-mate out in the middle of the night?"

Fred:	"That was on Okinawa. He was having a nightmare, and he was going to give our position away. So I knocked him out!"

Q:	"Did he realize in the morning what had happened?"

Fred.	"No, and I didn't tell him, either!"

Q:	"Weren't you declared missing-in-action sometime?"

Fred:    "No, I don't remember that.  One time I drove into the compound and a guy said, 'I thought you was dead!'  He was carrying the paperwork."

Q:        "Why did he think that?"

Fred:    "The truck in front of mine hit a mine and was blown up.  (Pause.)  It flipped completely over and landed on its wheels.  They thought it was my truck."

Q:        "Where--?"

Fred:    "Okinawa."

When we were looking at the pictures of the troop ship, I asked how long they were in those crowded conditions.  "That time--three weeks."  I said they obviously didn't have much to do.  "No.  They tried to get some close order drill going, but there wasn't room."  I said I suspected there might be a lack of enthusiasm for that.  "Right!"

I had not studied the war in the Pacific or the Korean War until I got Dad's notes to read.  (I didn't know they existed until the fall of 1988 and the spring of 1989.)  Primary sources, or eye-witness accounts, are so much more interesting than re-written, later accounts.  Readers are usually motivated to do more research on the incidents described, and that certainly worked in my case.  Of course, I have an advantage:  I work in a military library.  But I encourage other people to get their dads or uncles or grandpas to tell them about when and where they were, or to write down what they remember.  Then go to the local library or bookstore and see what you can find.  Some of the books I have listed in the bibliography are "in print," meaning you can still buy them.  Many of these books have bibliographies, or lists of other books and magazine articles.  Then go to the local library.  If it is a small public library, you may need to find a larger public library or a college/university library.  (But don't assume:  ask what they have or can get.)  Medium or large libraries will have a magazine index called <u>Reader's Guide to Periodical Literature</u> for the 1940s and 1950s.  This indexes news magazines such as <u>Time</u>, <u>Life</u>, and <u>Newsweek</u>, plus <u>National Geographic</u> (and other popular magazines).  If the library doesn't have the magazines you want, ask about Interlibrary Loan.  You will probably have to pay photocopy charges for magazine articles.  You can also request books on loan, and sometimes you have to pay postage or other fees.  Another source of information is the <u>New York Times Index</u>.  Most medium or large libraries have this, plus the newspaper on microfilm.

If you are a veteran of World War II or the Korean War, you probably won't learn all that much from my dad's book. You will probably say, "He didn't make it gruesome enough, and he didn't record the profanity." He did try to shield his family from the harsher aspects of what he experienced. If you want to read more realistic accounts, plenty are available. I feel this account is different from many because he did try to find things to relate which are not gruesome; he wasn't career; he wasn't infantry (even though all Marines are trained to fight, and they all get involved when necessary); he was enlisted. Many combat accounts are by infantry and/or officers.

The following bibliography lists only a few of the many books and magazines available. If you want to read more about the Marines, World War II, or the Korean War, these will get you started. If your library or book store doesn't have these--see what they do have!


Florence F. Klemm
Reference Librarian

III.	Bibliography of addition sources

These are just a few of the many items available on World War II, the Korean War, and the U.S.M.C.

WORLD WAR II: BOOKS:

Cass, Bevan G., ed. <u>History of the Six the Marine Division</u>. Washington: Infantry Journal Press, 1948.
> In addition to combat, this also covers training and occupation duty. Interesting photos, no index.

Costello, John. <u>The Pacific War 1941-1945</u>. NY: Quill, 1982.
> Large, detailed book which includes notes, bibliography, photos, maps, and an index. On p. 578, these statistics for the Battle of Okinawa are given: "Over 107,539 Japanese soldiers had died in battle and 27,769 were entombed in caves. . .an estimated 75,000 Okinawan civilians had become casualties. The land battle had cost the Americans over 7,374 dead and 31,807 wounded. At sea, the Japanese had lost 16 warships and over 800 planes, many of them Kamikazes. The 34 ships sunk by the Japanese suicide pilots--the 763 carrier planes lost, and the 4,907 American sailors killed--were the heaviest casualties inflicted by the Imperial Navy on the U.S. Navy in any battle of the entire war." On page 579, American casualties are estimated while making plans to invade Japan: ". . .at over the million mark." The dropping of the atom bomb made the invasion unnecessary.

Frank, Benis M., and Henry I. Shaw, Jr. <u>History of U.S. Marine Corps Operations in World War II, vol. 5: Victory and Occupation</u>. Washington, D.C.: Historical Branch, G-3 Division, Headquarters, U.S. Marine Corps, 1968.
> Includes Okinawa, the decision to drop the bomb, and occupation duty.

----------. <u>Okinawa: the Great Island Battle</u>. NY: Elsevier-Dutton, 1978.
> Includes photos, short bibliography, index.

Includes photos, short bibliography, index.

Galliant, T. Grady. <u>On Valor's Side</u>. Garden City: Doubleday, 1963.
> The author joined the Marines in 1941. He tells of his training and describes combat. Come quotes: ". . .the everyday language of the Corps is almost pure profanity. . ." (page xiii). On page 20: "Every Marine is a combat Marine." On page 302 he makes a statement which no doubt applied to later situations: "There is not a man in the First Marine Division who has not wondered why he survived; why it was he. . .and not some kind and good friend." On page 351: "It took us a long time to tell the difference between the training methods and actual warfare; there was some change, but not too much."

Manchester, William R. <u>Goodbye, Darkness; a Memoir of the Pacific War</u>. Boston: Little, Brown, 1980.
> The author was a Marine who participated in combat on Okinawa. Many years later, as a famous author, he returned to the island. War memories intermingled with modern sights.

Nichols, Chas. S., Jr., and Hentry I. Shaw, Jr. <u>Okinawa: Victory in the Pacific</u>. Historical Branch, G-3 Division, Headquarters, U.S. Marine Corps. Washington, D.C.: Government Printing Office, 1955.
> Illustrated with photos, this is the official history. Detailed maps are included at the back. Indexed.

Pyle, Ernie. <u>Ernie's War: the Best of Ernie Pyle's World War II Dispatches</u>. Edited with a biographical essay by David Nichols. NY: Random House, 1986.
> Journalist Pyle was much loved by the servicemen.

<u>Reader's Digest Illustrated Story of World War II</u>. Pleasantville, NY: The Reader's Digest Association, 1969.
> I found this one at a used book store, a good source for older books. The title describes the book.

Suizberger, C.L. <u>The American Heritage Picture History of</u>

<u>World War II</u>. NY: American Heritage/Bonanza Books, 1966.
> This large, fascinating book covers all war fronts, and, of course, has many photos.  Indexed.

U.S.M.C. <u>North China Pictorial</u>. Los Angeles: Pictorial California, 1946.
> Booklet of photos.

WORLD WAR II:  MAGAZINE ARTICLES

Army & Navy: Morale: <u>Time</u> 21 Jan 1946: 20-22.
> Most of the article is about the U.S. Army troops in Europe and the Philippines demonstrating to go home.  One section of the article is about the U.S. Marines in China.  For both soldiers and Marines, the "caste" system of privileges for officers hurt morale.  The troops also fail to see a need for their presence.  (The Marines did not demonstrate, however.)

Baldwin, Hanson W. "Okinawa: Victory at the Threshold." Pt. I. <u>Marine Corps Gazette</u> Dec. 1950: 40-47; Pt. II. Jan. 1951, 42-49.
> Exciting narration with emphasis on the Naval battle.

"Battle of the Pacific: Two Teams, One Goal." <u>Time</u> 11 June 1945: 30
> Continuing battle on Okinawa.

Duncan, David D. "Okinawa, Threshold to Japan." <u>National Geographic</u> Oct. 1945: 411-428
> Includes color photos of the island and natives.

"Ernie." <u>Time</u> 30 April 1945: 59
> Tribute to journalist Ernie Pyle, killed on Ie Jima, near Okinawa, 18 April 1945.  Photo.

"In Okinawa Mud." <u>Newsweek</u> 4 June 1945: 42
> Includes photos of combat.

"Insignia of the United States Armed Forces." <u>National Geographic</u> June, 1943: 651-748 (entire issue).
> Illustrated.

"Marines: the Housekeepers." <u>Time</u> 19 Nov. 1945: 26
        Marines in China.

"Pacific War: Savage Battles Continue as Europe's Peace
comes." <u>Life</u> 14 May 1945: 96-97
        Mainly Okinawa.

Yokoi, Toshiyuki. "Kamikazes and the Okinawa
Campaign." <u>United States Naval Institute Proceedings</u>
May 1954: 504-513.
        Author was an Admiral in the Imperial Japanese
        Navy.

KOREAN WAR: BOOKS

Blair, Clay. <u>The Forgotten War: American in Korea 1950-
1953</u>. NY: Doubleday, 1987.
        This book is primarily about the U.S. Army in
        Korea. It includes photos, notes, index. The
        author has some interesting things to say about
        President Truman.

Bok, Lee Suk. <u>The Impact of US Forces in Korea</u>.
Washington, D.C.: National Defense University Press,
1987.
        A history of the Korean War by a member of the
        ROK forces. Writing of the retreat from North
        Korea, he says: "Under severe weather
        conditions with temperatures 25 degrees below
        zero, with the threat of nine Chinese divisions
        near them, impossible road conditions. . .the
        Marine Division conducted its retirement
        successfully. . .The Marines crept, clawed, and
        fought their way, smashing road blocks, beating
        off attacks from either side (pages 50-51).

Hastings, Max. <u>The Korean War</u>. NY: Simon & Schuster,
1987.
        Includes diagrams, maps, photos, chronology,
        index.

Hopkins, William B. <u>One Bugle No Drums; the Marines at
Chosin Reservoir</u>. Chapel Hill: Algonquin Books of
Chapel Hill, 1986.
        The author was a Marine officer who participated

The author was a Marine officer who participated in the breakout from Chosin. This interesting book shows thought and research. The title refers to the bugle that plays taps for the men killed; the drums--or celebrations--are absent when the survivors return home.

Montross, Lynn, and Nicholas A. Canzona. <u>U.S. Marine Operations in Korea, 1950-1954</u>, vols 2-4. Washington, D.C.: Historical Branch, G-3, Headquarters U.S. Marine Corps, 1955-1962.
I used the maps in these books to standardize the spelling of the Korean towns in my dad's book. Of course, this is the official history and is detailed, with photos, maps, indexes, etc. The entire set has five volumes.

Truman, Harry S. <u>Public Papers of the Presidents of the United States: Harry S. Truman</u>. Containing the public messages, speeches, and statements of the president, January 1 to December 31, 1950. Washington D.C.: Government Printing Office, 1965.

----------. <u>Public Papers of the Presidents of the United States: Harry S. Truman</u>. Containing the public messages, speeches, and statements of the President, January 1 to December 31, 1951. Washington, D.C.: Government Printing Office, 1965.
President Truman had a great deal to say about Korea, the Marines, and General MacArthur.

KOREA: MAGAZINE ARTICLES

"Battle of Korea." <u>Time</u> 25 Dec 1950: 17-19.
Includes photos of withdrawal from North Korea.
"Battle of Korea: Dreadful Winter." <u>Time</u> 25 Sept 1950: 25-30
Talks about the cold.

"Battle of Korea: Over the Beaches." <u>Time</u> 25 Sep 1950: 25-30
The Marines land at Inchon. Photos.

"Call to Arms Against World Aggression." <u>Newsweek</u> 31 July 1950: 22-29

Doyle, James H., and Arthur J. Mayer. "December 1950 at Hungnam." <u>United States Naval Institute Proceedings</u> April 1979: 44-55.
> Evacuation of U.S. troops from North Korea after they escaped from Chinese troops. Photos.

Giusti, Ernest H. "Minute Men--1950 Model; the Reserves in Action." <u>Marine Corps Gazette</u> Sept 1951: 22-31
> Photos of departures from various cities.

Griffin, William G.K. "Typhoon at Kobe." <u>Marine Corps Gazette</u> Sept 1951: 60-65.
> The invasion fleet being loaded for the Inchon landing was almost destroyed by a typhoon. Men were living aboard some of the ships because lack of space for them on shore. (My dad enjoyed reading this.)

"How U.S. Cities Can Prepare for Atomic War." <u>Life</u> 18 Dec. 1950: 76-86.

Keene, R.R. "A Division Surrounded." <u>Leatherneck</u> Nov 1990: 34-43.
> First Marine Division in North Korea, 40 years ago.

Keene, R.R. "The Division Breaks Out." <u>Leatherneck</u> Dec 1990: 20-29.
> Descriptive article of combat and cold weather.

"Men at War: the First Team." <u>Time</u> 14 Aug 1950: 16-20.
> Marines arrive in Pusan, Korea. Article gives some history of the Marines, especially in WWII. Includes color photos of Korea.

Moffett, Hugh. "The Situation in a Nutshell: 'Bug Out.'" <u>Life</u> 18 Dec 1950: 28-31.
> U.N. troops leave North Korea, but so do many Koreans.

Montross, Lynn, and Norman W. Hicks. "They Were There." <u>Leatherneck</u> pt 1: Dec 1960: 48-53; pt 2: Jan 1961: 48-53.
> The authors sent questionnaires to Marine

veterans who were in Korea in 1950. The articles contain memories of these men. Both articles have photographs.

Nakkula, Al. "Families Weep as Denver Marines Entrain; First Reserve Unit in Colorado Answers Call to Colors. <u>Rocky Mountain News</u> 3 Aug 1950: 5+
Describes ceremony for departing Marines. Photos.

"New United Nations Line--MacArthur's." <u>Newsweek</u> 9 Oct 1950: 19-25.
Includes several other sub-divided articles on the Korean War. Photos, map.

"Once More 'We Got a Hell of a Beating.'" <u>Life</u> 11 Dec 1950: 32-45.
Discusses North Korea in 1950: 25-below zero weather; Chinese entry into the war. Also covers President Truman's announcement that use of the atomic bomb was an option.

"Retreat of the 20,000." <u>Time</u> 18 Dec. 1950: 26-31.
"It was an epic of great suffering and great valor."

"Speaking of Pictures; a Determined Marine Does A Strip Tease in Reverse in Korean Winter Uniforms." <u>Look</u> 27 Nov. 1950: 14-15.
Eleven photos showing the various layers of winter uniforms for Marines in Korea.

Tallent, Robert. "Korean Life Line." <u>Leatherneck</u> July 1951: 14-21+.
Story and photos on the Motor Transport units in Korea. Includes photo of a mobile machine shop.

"There Was A Christmas In Korea." <u>Life</u> 25 Dec. 1950: 8-19.
Photos of retreat by David Douglas Duncan.

"War in Asia." <u>Time</u> 9 Oct. 1950: 26-34.
Now that the Korean War is almost over, where will the U.S. next fight Communism?

"We Walk, Not Run, To Exit." <u>Life</u> 8 Jan. 1951: 15-19
>Subtitle: "X Corps Evacuates Hungnam to Fight Again In The South." Photos by David D. Duncan.

"Where the Red Shadow Fell; North Korea's Liberated Capital Shows the Signs of Russian Rule." <u>Life</u> 27 Nov. 1950: 56-58.
>Shows Soviet posters, murals, etc. in Pyongyang.

KOREAN WAR: OTHER MATERIALS

<u>Korea: the Forgotten War</u>. Videotape hosted by Robert Stack. Los Angeles: Fox Hills Video, 1987.

U.S. Dept. of State. <u>Background Notes: South Korea</u>. Washington, D.C.: GPO, 1987.

GENERAL INFORMATION: BOOKS

Coletta, Paolo E. <u>An Annotated Bibliography of U.S. Marine Corps History</u>. NY: University Press of America, 1986.
>Several of the books and articles in my bibliography are from this one.

----------, ed. <u>United States Navy and Marine Corps Bases, Domestic</u>. Westport: Greenwood Press, 1985.
>Gives history and description of each base. Bibliography included at the end of each article.

Gaynor, Frank, ed. <u>The New Military and Naval Dictionary</u>. NY: Philosophical Library, 1951.
>I used this to verify the spelling of military terms used by my dad.

Heinl, Robert Debs, Jr. <u>Handbook for Marine NCOs</u>. 3rd ed. Annapolis: Naval Institute Press, 1988.
>Gives history and organization of the USMC. Describes uniforms, training, etc.

<u>Jane's Fighting Ships, 1950-51</u>. NY: McGraw-Hill, 1950.
>I used this to identify the destroyer photo which my dad took on the way home from Korea. The Jane Publishing Co. has several valuable sets in addition to the set on ships: aircraft, weapon

systems, infantry weapons, etc.

Johnson, Richard S. <u>How to Locate Anyone Who Is Or Has Been In The Military</u>. 5th ed. Burlington, N.C.: MIE Publishing, 1992.
> Small book which lists base locators, various service groups, etc.

Millett, Allan R. <u>Semper Fidelis; The History of the United States Marine Corps</u>. NY: Macmillan, 1980.

Parker, William D. <u>A Concise History of the United States Marine Corps. 1775-1969</u>. Washington, D.C.: Historical Division, Headquarters, United States Marine Corps, 1970.

Pick, Albert. <u>Standard Catalog of World Paper Money</u>, 5th ed. 2 vols. Iola, Wisc.: Krause, 1986.
> I used this to identify the paper money my dad sent home.

Riley, David L. <u>Uncommon Valor...Decorations, Badges, and Service Medals of the U.S. Navy and Marine Corps</u>. Hopkinsville, KY: Eagle Print Shop, 1980.
> Color photos of medals, ribbons, insignia. Narration explains qualifications for various awards.

GENERAL INFORMATION: OTHER MATERIALS

"Armed Forces Decorations and Awards." Washington, D.C.: GPO, 1967. (DOD P-17B)
> Chart which illustrates ribbons and medals. Gives reference to regulations for each service.

Marine Corps Historical Center, Washington Navy Yard, Bldg. 58, Washington, D.C. 20374.
> Includes museum, library, gift shop. The library includes a collection of personal papers. The gift shop is run by the Marine Corps Historical Foundation.

Naval Personnel Records Center, 9700 Page Boulevard, St. Louis, MO 63132.
> Government agency which can supply military records to veterans or next of kin of deceased veterans. Write for a form. Not all service

records are here; the form gives more information on other locations.

Sgt. Sylvester Antolak

Aboard the Antolak

Tugboat

Sanpan

Fire boat, greeting the returning Marines